RACE AND ASSESSMENT IN
HIGHER EDUCATION

RACE AND ASSESSMENT IN HIGHER EDUCATION

From Conceptualising Barriers to Making Measurable Change

BY

PAUL IAN CAMPBELL
University of Leicester, UK

United Kingdom – North America – Japan
India – Malaysia – China

Emerald Publishing Limited
Emerald Publishing, Floor 5, Northspring, 21-23 Wellington Street, Leeds
LS1 4DL

First edition 2024

Copyright © 2024 Paul Ian Campbell.
Published under exclusive licence by Emerald Publishing Limited.

Reprints and permissions service
Contact: www.copyright.com

No part of this book may be reproduced, stored in a retrieval system, transmitted in any form or by any means electronic, mechanical, photocopying, recording or otherwise without either the prior written permission of the publisher or a licence permitting restricted copying issued in the UK by The Copyright Licensing Agency and in the USA by The Copyright Clearance Center. Any opinions expressed in the chapters are those of the authors. Whilst Emerald makes every effort to ensure the quality and accuracy of its content, Emerald makes no representation implied or otherwise, as to the chapters' suitability and application and disclaims any warranties, express or implied, to their use.

British Library Cataloguing in Publication Data
A catalogue record for this book is available from the British Library

ISBN: 978-1-83549-743-2 (Print)
ISBN: 978-1-83549-740-1 (Online)
ISBN: 978-1-83549-742-5 (Epub)

INVESTOR IN PEOPLE

CONTENTS

List of Abbreviations — vii

Acknowledgements — ix

1. Introduction — 1

Part 1: Exploring the Lived Experiences of Race and Assessment in HE

2. White British Students' Experiences of Assessment — 17
3. Black British Students' Experiences of Assessment — 35
4. British South Asian Students' Experiences of Assessment — 49
5. Conceptualising Inter- and Intra- Race-Based Barriers in Assessment — 59

Part 2: What Difference Does Racially Inclusive Assessment Make, and For Who?

6. The Effects of Racially Inclusive Assessment on the Race Award Gap and on Students' Lived Experiences of Assessment — 73
7. Racially Inclusive Assessment and Academic Teaching Staff — 101
8. Discussion and Concluding Comments — 115

Afterword: 12 Years a Black Race Inclusion Academic – Some Reflections on Working in a *Postracism* Space — 133

Appendix. 'Policy Shorts': Mapping and 'Tackling' Racial Inequities in HE Assessment – Summarising the Case Study — 151

References	*175*
Index	*185*

LIST OF ABBREVIATIONS

AFL—Assessment for Learning
APP—Access and Participation Plan
FE—Further Education
FIF—First in Family
HE—Higher Education
HEP—Higher Education Provider
OFS—Office for Students
PrAS—Pre-Assessment Support
QAA—Quality Assurance Agency
RAG—Race Award Gap
RIPIAG—Racially Inclusive Practice in Assessment Guidance Intervention
STEM—Science, Technology, Engineering and Mathematics
TASO—The Centre for Transforming Access and Student Outcomes

ACKNOWLEDGEMENTS

This book is for all students of colour and students from marginalised backgrounds in higher education. For whom, changing the academe into a space that works equally for you has taken – and is taking – far too long.

I also need to thank Ben, Bernadine, Beth, Gary, Chloe, Graham, Sadiya and everyone else who has supported this work over the last 5 years. I am truly indebted to you all.

1

INTRODUCTION

At the most rudimentary level, this book has two objectives: (1) to sketch out the assessment experiences of British-born undergraduate students of colour compared to their White peers, and (2) to provide an account of the measurable quantitative and qualitative effects of making assessment more racially inclusive on undergraduate students' and staffs' experiences in HE.

In doing so, this monograph is different from the majority of current education and sociology books that are focused on inclusion. It is not simply about providing a 'thick' description of a problem and using social theory to make sense of it (this is of course a noble objective in its own right, but too often seems to be the finish line for many education and inclusion-based studies). This book does more. It also provides you, the reader, with empirically substantiated guidance for what works in addressing the problem. In this case, it tells you how and why the experience of assessment is unequal for global majority undergraduate students in the UK *and* what we can do to change it. But this leads us to an obvious and important question, which might even be the initial reason why some of you picked up this book in the first place: What has race got to do with assessment? In my experience of leading race inclusion change across the higher education sector for the last half-decade, this is a surprisingly common question that must be addressed here at the outset. My own story is a useful place to attempt to formulate the answer.

My parents relocated to the United Kingdom from Jamaica in the 1960s. They were part of the movement of thousands of young British citizens from the Caribbean who answered the call to help rebuild the 'mother country', which had been quite literally battered by the Third Reich. Upon arrival, however, the Black women and men from the Caribbean faced blanket processes of race-based structural ghettoisations predominantly in employment and housing (Campbell, 2016). Their children faced structural and overt racisms in the British education system, which formally and informally classified them as educationally 'subnormal' (Wallace & Joseph-Salisbury, 2021).

This backcloth meant that I, like many Black children during the 1970s and 1980s, grew up in a working-class household located in a socioeconomically challenged and racially diverse inner-urban locale. In my case, this was an East London Borough called Newham, which since the 1980s has been one of the country's most racially diverse wards. This meant that my time in compulsory education was spent in classrooms with student populations where people of colour were the numerical majority. This was, however, where the racial diversity that characterised my early educative experiences started *and stopped*. For example, during my time in infant, primary and secondary school, I was taught by 4 Head Teachers, 3 Deputy Head Teachers, 10 Heads of Year and Deputy Heads of Year, 11 Form Tutors, 46 classrooms teachers and 10 teachers who doubled as sports-coaches. Out of the 84 teachers who spanned my 11 years in compulsory education, only 3 were people of colour. In addition to this, a largely racially intolerant education system and a predominantly middle-class, White and Eurocentric curriculum meant there were few opportunities to relate the education that I received to my own life and cultural identity in the same way that many of my White peers could.

These cleavages between my own biography and the educational diet offered, contributed to a general sense of disaffection throughout my school years. It, ultimately, culminated with me leaving compulsory education having sat only two GCSE exams and with no formal qualifications. This was despite the fact that I was in all 'top set' classes and frequently described by my teachers as 'extremely bright' – albeit seemingly uninterested in my studies (This was an apt observation, I might add).

Returning to education to study sociology as a mature student of colour, nearly a decade later in 2003, little appeared to have changed in relation to the general Whiteness that characterised the British education system, the curriculum (in HE), and assessment processes. During 7 years as an undergraduate and postgraduate student, for example, I was never taught by a single person of colour. Moreover, despite its claims to explore aspects of our social identities such as gender, class, and race, there were few opportunities to relate, read about or apply my undergraduate training and burgeoning sociological imagination to my own lived experiences as a Black and working-class student in either the course readings, content, practice, *or assessment*.

In most cases, the faculty of educators that taught me possessed neither the racial diversity, racial literacy and/or the race-based pedagogical training to help me synthesise my general sociological training through the prism of race, class and late-modern Britain. My learning in HE took place at what I describe as an 'epistemological distance' (Campbell, 2022a, 2023). Put simply, for the most part, I had to learn about other people and from the perspective of other people.

In addition to this, and perhaps the most challenging aspect of this situation for me, was that when it came to 'doing' assessments, I had to construct answers to examinations and tests in ways that resonated and fitted with the Eurocentric world view of a White faculty, whose understandings of academic excellence, rigour and 'accepted' knowledge were often the product of their own raced and classed biographies and their location in the global north. This experience of assessment was expertly explained by the African Caribbean heritage, Labour MP, Dawn Butler (2023), who recalled that she once failed an oral presentation, because her White British teacher did not believe her that cockroaches could fly. She explains that she would have passed the presentation if her teacher's own knowledge base extended beyond the confines of the White British experience. Put another way, if her teacher was not White and born in the UK but was Black and raised in the Caribbean, they would have known that Dawn's story was true. *In Jamaica, cockroaches fly*! Like Dawn, my eventual successes in assessment and in education in HE more widely took place in spite of, and not because of, my undergraduate sociology training.

Research on the sociology of race, inclusion and education demonstrates how these experiences described here were not localised to me, or to Britain in the 1980s, 1990s and early 2000s. *The Guardian* newspaper, for example, reported that a 2023 study by Durham University found that students of colour are still unlikely to be taught by at least one teacher who 'looks like them' during their entire time in compulsory education (Ofori, 29 August 2023). My own work (Campbell, 2016, 2020; Campbell et al., 2021) and that of others, such as Wallace (2017), Bhopal and Myers (2023), and Advance HE (2021), make transparent how the experience described above still characterises the educative experiences of many students of colour in HE today, and manifests in unequal experiences of happiness and belonging.

The academe has been sensitive to *some* of the processes that I describe above. For example, significant attention has been given to the effects of studying a White and Eurocentric curriculum on differences in degree award outcomes and satisfaction between White and Black and racially minoritised students in higher education (see TASO, 2022a). However, seldom has attention been given specifically to the ways in which assessment is experienced unevenly by students of colour compared to White peers. This is despite assessment being arguably one of the most crucial of processes in education that determine student successes, failures and future opportunities for social mobility. Put another way, seldom has scholarly attention been given to critically examining the place of assessment within the colonial systems, processes and practices that impact unevenly on undergraduate students of colour. Neither has it been given to providing empirically substantiated guidance to help educators identify and mitigate these processes within their practice. This book is the first sociological case study to respond directly to this absence.

To achieve this, this case study draws on qualitative and quantitative data gleaned from two large three-year projects. The first, explored the contrasting experiences of assessment between students of colour and White peers and used this to develop the

Racially Inclusive Assessment Guidance. This was 20 recommendations for making assessment practice more racially inclusive. The second, developed the *Racially Inclusive Assessment Guidance* into the *Racially Inclusive Practice in Assessment Guidance Intervention* (RIPIAG). The intervention consisted of 4 practice-based teaching resources that were designed to be embedded into undergraduate modules (see Chapter 6 for full details). This study evaluated the effectiveness of the RIPIAG for improving the lived and everyday experiences of assessment for students of colour, and for reducing the race award gap that exists in assessment outcomes between students of colour and White peers, across three UK Higher Education Providers (HEPs). This project was generously sponsored by the Quality Assurance Agency's (QAA's) Collaborative Enhancement Fund. The combined studies included focus group and semi-structured interviews with over 111 undergraduate students and 7 teaching staff, and the assessment performance data of over 175 undergraduate students.

Drawing on this body of research, this book represents an original and world-leading contribution to the discussion on race and education in three novel ways: (1) It is the first to empirically map the contrasting experiences and barriers experienced by British students of colour in assessment in UK HEPs. (2) It is the first to use these experiences to provide practitioners, policymakers and general audiences with empirically substantiated guidance on what works in relation to best practice in racially inclusive assessment. (3) It is the first scholarly work to offer an empirical account that details the impact of making assessment racially inclusive on racially minoritised students' qualitative experiences of assessment, and to equalising the quantitative race award gaps that they currently experience.

In sum, this monograph provides a much-needed starting point for a more meaningful and empirically substantiated discussion of what works and in what ways with regards to tackling race-based inequities in assessment. It is for educationalists, scholars, policymakers and anyone who is interested in how education works unevenly for people of colour in the UK and importantly, for those who want to know how to go about making assessment and HE more equitable for all. It is ultimately for those who endeavour to see students of colour succeed because of, and not in spite of, how assessment and related practices work in HE.

ATTEMPTS TO CLOSE THE RACE AWARD GAP

Nationally in 2020, the aggregate race award gap (henceforth RAG) between the percentage of domicile undergraduate students of colour and their White peers achieving a 'good degree' (2.1 or above) in the UK was 9.9% (see Advance HE, 2021). Influenced by the Office for Students' (OFS's) decision to place the responsibility of addressing the RAG on individual HEPs in 2018, the last half a decade has seen the sector largely respond with efforts to neutralise the racial inequalities that manifest in course content or to 'decolonise' their curricula. This was also influenced by what Codiroli-McMaster (2021) describes as an empirically unsubstantiated academic consensus, which holds that making taught curricula more racially inclusive will directly reduce the RAG (Advance HE, 2021; Arday et al., 2020). One consequence of the sector's laser-like focus on curricula is that thus far, seldom have assessment and related practices been meaningfully explored as part of the processes that exclude students of colour and contribute to the RAG (Campbell et al., 2021).

My seminal report for the Centre for Transforming Access and Student Outcomes (TASO, 2022a) on the effects of making curricula racially inclusive underscores the importance of race-inclusion work focused on curricula *in a general sense*. Importantly, I also recommend caution for using this approach as a *sole or specific* response to RAGs (Campbell et al., 2022). The findings indicated that interventions aimed at pluralising course content are effective for increasing the quantitative levels of student satisfaction recorded in module evaluations. They are also efficacious for enhancing the relevance of course materials to the lives of students of colour and for improving their qualitative senses of belonging on their degree programmes. However, the findings also showed that the curricula-based intervention was less effective for directly reducing RAGs in a quantitatively significant way. In turn, I concluded that 'tackling' the racial exclusions and barriers that manifest specifically within assessments were likely to be more directly impactful for achieving this outcome. Thus far, this book is the first case study to test this assertion.

ASSESSMENT, RACE AND RACE AWARD GAPS

What do we know about how race-based barriers in assessment contribute to the race award gap in HE, so far? There is a burgeoning body of work that points to a direct causal relationship between assessment and related practices and the RAG in a general sense. Singh et al. (2022, p. 229), for example, proffer that UK HEPs are directly responsible for the RAG, and particularly through their 'discriminatory styles of assessment and marking and insufficient support from scholars who can be biased' against students of colour (see also Bunce et al., 2021; Mountford-Zimdars et al., 2015). Cramer (2021) points to the overuse of particular forms of assessment as another causal factor for the RAG in Science, Technology, Engineering and Mathematics (STEM)-based subjects. She elucidates that students of colour do not perform as well in exams as they do in coursework and thus, the alacrity of STEM subjects to employ exams as their primary mode of assessment contributes greatly to this situation.

The RAG and race-based inequities in assessment in particular are also influenced by racialised inequities within the wider educative experiences of undergraduate students in UK HEPs. Khuda and Kamruzzaman (2021), for example, highlight how a lack of racial diversity in course reading lists and materials place non-White students at a disadvantage in assessment (see also Abu Moghli & Kadiwal, 2021; Arday et al., 2020). Rana et al. (2022) draw attention to the role of academics within assessment inequity. They assert that the general lack of racial literacy and awareness of their own unconscious racial biases among teaching staff in HE directly contributes to minority ethnic students' under and unequal performances in assessment – and to the RAG more widely.

Pointing to a lack of empirically substantiated explorations into the causes of RAGs and into what works for mitigating them, Codiroli-McMaster (2021) argues that much of what the academe currently knows about the relationship between race, assessment and RAGs are drawn from academic assumptions – and not from empirically substantiated interventions or evaluative data. This position is contrasted with a growing body of work and activity that have begun to map the causes – and offer some empirically substantiated solutions – for inequalities in assessment in relation to other protected characteristics and social divisions, such as social class, disability, mental health and (class-related) language barriers within HE assessment (Advance HE, 2022; Bianco, 2022; Hockings, 2010; TASO, 2022a).

The theme of assessment has featured, to varying degrees, as a part of the broader conversation on the experience of students of colour in UK HEPs. For example, studies have examined the influence of teacher (racial) bias(es) and stereotyping (Burgess & Greaves, 2013), Whiteness (Bhopal, 2018), and lower teacher expectations and lower feelings of belonging when compared to White students, on students of colour's assessment performances and outcomes (see MacNell et al., 2015). Cousin and Cureton (2012) and Hinton and Higson (2017) have both highlighted the limited efficacy of 'anonymous' marking policies in mitigating the impact of these processes on assessment and degree outcomes. However, at the time of writing, there exists little empirical data on the ways in which assessment is experienced unevenly by students of colour or on why this inequity occurs. There is also a lack of evaluative work on the effectiveness of interventions for *measurably* improving the assessment experience of minority ethnic students in UK HEPs or for reducing the award gap. To our knowledge, this book is the first to provide a direct and empirically substantiated response to these gaps in the canon. To achieve these three objectives, the book is organised in the following way.

STRUCTURE OF THE BOOK

To achieve the first two objectives, the first part of the book (*Chapters 2, 3 and 4*) deals with the following more specific research questions: What are the disaggregated assessment experiences of students of colour in UK HEPs, how are these complicated by race and how might these contribute to, or produce wider, outcome differences in awards between them and their White peers? Why do certain racially minoritised students, on average, appear to have differing and uneven experiences of inclusion in certain forms of assessment over others? To what extent are issues of accessibility and inclusion in assessment for minority ethnic students intrinsic to specific assessment types or connected to wider pedagogical practice? How do wider social and cultural factors – and proxies for race – such as socio-economic background, cultural capital, location and so on, intersect, influence and contribute to uneven experiences (and in turn performances) in particular forms of assessment?

In turn, Chapters 2, 3 and 4 present the lived stories and experiences of assessment for British White, Black and South Asian undergraduate students, respectively, who all study Biology, Law, Sociology and Physics at one Higher Education Provider, The University of Bourne (this is a pseudonym). Each chapter provides a 'thick' description of each group of students' contrasting experiences of (particular forms) of HE assessment and of related assessment practices, such as their ability to access support prior to and after their assessment. They also sketch out each student groups' differing experiences of overt and covert forms of race and intersected discriminations. Finally, they trace some of the ways in which these experiences differ between, and within, larger and more generalised racial categories, along the axes of class, religion and diaspora.

Chapter 5 provides a discussion which theoretically conceptualises these racialised experiences of assessment. In doing so, it provides an expanded and theoretical frame to make sense of the unifying and contrasting experiences of assessment that exist across the three student groups, and uses this to formulate a number of recommendations for best race inclusion in assessment practice (which are in turn used to produce the RIPIAG that is tested in the second half of the monograph).

The second part of this book sketches out the impact of the RIPIAG's capacity to improve students from minority ethnic backgrounds' lived experiences of assessment, and its capacity to improve/develop/progress the levels of racial literacy and understanding of racial inequities in assessment among teaching staff.

Specifically, Chapter 6 deals with the first two tests. It begins by reporting on the quantitative effects of the RIPIAG on reducing the award gaps reported on the treated modules across 3 HEPs. These results are then compared and contrasted with a 'thick description' of the measurable changes brought about by the intervention on the students from racialised backgrounds' lived and everyday experiences of assessment.

Chapter 7 centres the experiences of the teaching staff who piloted the intervention. Importantly, it does two things here. Firstly, it examines the value and limitations of the intervention for improving HE staffs' racial literacy. Secondly, it provides a comparative narrative viewpoint of the impact of the intervention on their students' experiences, attitudes and approaches to assessment.

Chapter 8 concludes the book with a theoretical discussion which consists of three specific conversations. Firstly, it connects the findings to the more general discussion of race, and to race in education in Britain, and spells out some of the ways this case study contributes to this broader conversation. Secondly, it provides a specific response to the three broad objectives of the book (that is, to shed light on the unequal experiences of assessment for British-born undergraduate students of colour when compared to White British students and to explain why these inequities occur. And to sketch out the measurable quantitative and qualitative effects of making assessment more racially inclusive for (all) undergraduate students and their teachers). Thirdly, it discusses the ways in which current assessment practices reward and marginalise the currencies, hegemonies and habitus' unevenly clustered around certain raced and ethnic communities in the UK. This provides the basis to discuss the usefulness and limitations of using interventions for addressing the race award gap that are only focused on addressing barriers that exist within specific and singular areas of education, such as those that are manifest in assessment or within curricula, for example.

The book closes with an Afterword. This chapter is a personal reflection on my 12 years as a Black man in the academe and on my

Introduction

last 5 years as a leader in HE and leading voice in relation to race equity work. I share and triangulate my own experiences of racial inclusion and exclusion within the academe with some of the experiences detailed within this book and with the experience of race in HE more widely. I draw on all this to make the case for the need for a new '*pos*tracism' theoretical framework to make sense of the apparent inclusion/exclusion juxtapositions that characterise many of the experiences of race in contemporary HE. One which allows us to move beyond seeing and understanding this as solely an experience which is contradictory or conflicting.

The Appendix contains a 'Policy Shorts' Chapter. This short chapter is explicitly for policymakers and educationalists. It provides a succinct summary of the book's recommendations and key takeaways. It also signposts the reader to the specific findings/conclusions from which the recommendations and takeaways are generated. The chapter concludes by providing the reader with clear guidance on how to measure the effectiveness of each recommendation if they were to implement them into their own practice/environ.

METHODOLOGY

Before our attention turns to tracing the experiences of race and assessment, it is important to end this chapter by saying something about the philosophical position adopted and in turn the methodological choices taken, when putting this study together.

To map the students' experiences of assessment, a qualitative approach was employed for the following philosophical reasons. The lived experiences of minority ethnic groups in (social and) educational environs and processes, such as assessment, are ontologically fluid and thus, often inadequately captured by quantitative data (Campbell, 2020; Wallace, 2017). The consensus among race interested scholars, such as Gunaratnam (2003), is that to obtain a critical comprehension of minority ethnic students' experiences in education, researchers should also employ qualitative approaches, such as in-depth questioning (Campbell, 2016). Moreover, we must avoid aggregating the educative experiences of students from separate minority ethnic communities (Campbell, 2020).

Mindful of these important theoretical, methodological and sampling considerations, the data examined in *Chapters 2, 3 and 4* are drawn from twelve focus groups interviews, and 6 one-to-one semi-structured interviews with undergraduate, and alumni students, respectively. A purposive sampling method was used and resulted in 44 undergraduate student-participants studying on 4 purposefully selected courses at the University of Bourne (Biology, Physics, Law and Sociology). Focus groups were organised around their disciplines and three broad ethnic categories (1: African and African-Caribbean heritage, 2: British South-Asian heritage and 3: White British).

The evaluation of the RIPIAG that is explored in *Chapters 6 and 7* employed a 'mixed' quantitative and qualitative approach. Positivist approaches and quantitative-based examinations are especially useful in education-based studies that seek to numerically capture, examine or evaluate the relationship between one variable or intervention (such as an intervention for making assessment racially inclusive) on other variables – in this case, the performance of students of colour in assessment. As outlined above, trying to capture the *lived* and everyday experience of race and exclusion in assessment and related practice is widely accepted as being ontologically problematic if solely an objectivist, and, in turn, positivistic approach is utilised. According to Solomos (2003), for example, racialised identities and experiences are widely recognised as dynamic and not necessarily salient at all times. The consequence of this for research is that they exist beyond the scope of quantitative measurements alone (Wallace, 2017).

In line with this consensus, it was obvious that if I wanted to gain a critical understanding and measurable impact of this intervention on improving the lived experience of race and education and for reducing the RAG, respectively, I had to utilise qualitative approaches, such as in-depth questioning *in addition* to quantitative data sets.

The RIPIAG was trialed between September 2021 and December 2022, in 6 modules, across 3 partner HEPs: University of Bourne, Meadow University and Wiseman University (all pseudonyms), of which 1 was research intensive and 2 were teaching focused. The sample consisted of 175 undergraduate students and 7 module leaders (at least 35% of learners in each module were domicile undergraduate students of colour). Colleagues at partner institutions self-selected a module or modules from a course or courses to trial the intervention. Modules selected were at the discretion of the partner HEP. However, for validity purposes, all modules consisted of at least 25 students, of which at least 30% had to be students of colour.

Quantitative data consisted of the assessment performance scores of undergraduate students taken from the treated undergraduate modules. Only one module could be selected for each level on a particular degree programme. For example, a HEP could only select one module from their portfolio of modules at level 1 on their sociology degree. This was to ensure that comparative data gleaned from students' experiences of, and performances in, their assessments in the other modules that they studied at that level could be generated.

Qualitative data were drawn from a total of 12 focus group interviews with 60 purposively selected current undergraduate students and the module leaders of the selected modules. The students in our sample self-defined according to three different broad ethnic communities (1: African and African-Caribbean heritage (14), 2: British South Asian heritage (17) and 3: White British (29)). Where possible, focus groups were organised along these ethnicity themes. Interview data were drawn primarily from semi-structured interviews with module convenors.

In both phases of the project (the mapping of students' experiences of assessment and assessing the impact of the intervention of students' experiences of, and performances in, assessment), the inclusion of White student perspectives provided an important data set for 'comparison, contrast and methodological triangulation during various parts of the narrative' (see Campbell, 2020, p. 12). The employment of these mechanisms for sampling, triangulation and validation enabled me to track the reoccurring and key patterns of correlation and divergence across, and within, the experiences of students from different raced backgrounds, and enabled the production of a robust narrative, respectively (Arksey & Knight, 1999).

Interviews and focus groups were transcribed verbatim, and all qualitative data coded, and key words extrapolated and collated. Emergent themes were identified through a process of 'pattern coding', where coded data are reconfigured into more compact and meaningful groupings. All data were anonymised, and pseudonyms were used in place of students', faculty members' and HEPs' real names and other signposts, in accordance with the ethical guidelines set out by my university's ethics committee.

So that explains what this book is about. Why it is important. How I conducted the research and why I chose to do it in this way. Job done. It is to present the key themes that emerged from the students' accounts of assessment that our attention now turns.

PART 1

EXPLORING THE LIVED EXPERIENCES OF RACE AND ASSESSMENT IN HE

2

WHITE BRITISH STUDENTS' EXPERIENCES OF ASSESSMENT

What are the assessment experiences of White undergraduate students studying Biology, Law, Sociology and Physics? How do they align and differ, and why? This chapter seeks to open up discussion on these points. Before I do this, however, perhaps I should address what might be an 'elephant in the room' for some readers. That is that it may seem a little peculiar to begin an exploration of race and assessment by tracing the experiences of British-born students who self-describe as being 'White'.

This confusion often derives from an assumption that White communities are race*less* and, by extension, the de-facto 'normal' experience. This is a false presumption. The experience of White and middle-classed individuals and communities *are highly racialised*. Let us take, for example, scholarly works that examine the different aspects of our social realities and cultures, such as gender, disability, youth cultures, cultural capital, taste, culture, pastimes and so on. All are explored from a White perspective *unless otherwise explicitly stated*. To test this reality, simply consider if we were to sociologically explore any of these aspects of our social realities in relation to how they are experienced by global majority communities in the UK, then we would *have to* preface each study with a reference to the specific raced community with which we were concerned. Either Black, South Asian, East Asian and so forth.

The expectation is that unless otherwise stated, we are discussing social phenomena from a 'White' racialised perspective. This is an important concept to grasp especially as the goal of this book is to understand the relationship between race and education and related practices.

Moncrieffe (2020, p. 29) asserts that the White secondary-school teachers he surveyed possessed their own specific race and classed 'cultural backgrounds, values, customs, perceptions and prejudices'. He elucidates that these aspects of the teachers' social make up are not left at the door when they enter the classroom. Instead, they play an 'important' and 'influential role in teaching situations'. They also and often influence the cultural outputs in these spaces, such as the exercises, machinery and practices that are used to test students. They also influence the currencies, experiences and understandings that teachers expect their students to possess in order to pass them.

Moncrieffe's observations were rehearsed (to an extent) in the findings of sociolinguists Ahmend and Cushing (2021), who observed that assessment and related practices in HE are also constructed around who and what educational gatekeepers' imagine constitute the typical, 'standard' or 'ideal' university student (Of course, teachers of colour can also subscribe or conform to these racialised hegemonies that are in operation in White sub-cultural environs, see Campbell 2020).

This ideal student fantasy held within the academe is usually reflective of, and influenced by, the race(d) and class(ed) identities of educational gatekeepers who, as Fletcher (2010) points out, cannot escape their own biographies. In many ways, this is a process whereby the White hegemon (re)imagines and reproduces the White hegemon. The potential consequence of this situation for students whose biographies fall outside of this narrow race and classed (and gendered, and so forth) construction is that their lived realities are not meaningfully accounted for in assessment and related activities, policy, practice or support provisions – as well as in HE policy more widely.

Conversely, students whose identities align with these fantasies are more likely to find 'education' significantly easier to access and navigate. It is for this reason that in our attempt to understand how and why assessment works differently for students from different raced backgrounds, we begin with the assessment experiences of students whose biographies are the closest to the gatekeepers' imagined ideal student, as our starting and reference point.

WHITE STUDENTS' EXPERIENCES IN, AND PREFERENCES FOR, DIFFERENT MODES OF ASSESSMENT

I really like the lab reports because, [as] I think Participant One touched on it earlier, you do the hands-on experiment and then you write about your experience doing it. It's a lot easier to write about something you've done, rather than them just giving you a question, and being like, oh write an article about this. (Siobhan, White Biology Student)

For me, the 3000- or 4000-word essays [are best]. I like doing them. They're long enough that you can get out all you want to say, and you've got enough time because it's coursework. (Sarah, White Sociology Student)

I think exams [are my favourite assessment type]. I've been doing them all through school up until now. It's a very familiar process. Whereas report writing, I think I'm still working out exactly what's expected of me when it comes to doing them. (Kel, White Physics Student)

The broad spectrum of assessment preferences exampled in the three students' testimonies above introduce a key feature of the assessment experiences for the White student participants in this study. That is, for the most part, they generally found all forms of assessment accessible and to varying degrees enjoyable. This did not mean that they did not have preferences for some forms of assessment over others. They did. There were clear patterns of preferences in different disciplines. But, for the most part, preferences for this group of students appeared to be influenced by what we might describe as pedagogy-related factors or by feelings of comfort when taking certain forms of assessment, which were either linked to a greater familiarity with that type of test or because the assignment was seen to align with what they perceived to be their own innate strengths or 'natural' ways of learning. As demonstrated above by a student who succinctly put it, that when it came to exams: 'It's not even that I can't do exams, because I can. I have got a good memory. I just don't enjoy them'.

For most White biology students, exams and continuous forms of assessment were most popular because regular testing was claimed to help them keep up to date with module content and to stay on top of their studies. For White sociology students, essays and coursework were most popular, due to this format providing them with what they felt was the most space to fully express ideas and subject knowledge.

White physics students showed the strongest preference for (standard and multiple-choice) exams and open book assessment formats when compared to physics students from Black and South Asian backgrounds. This appeared to be due to a greater familiarity with, and prior knowledge of, standard format exams accrued during their time in compulsory or further education. The same preference and rationale were proffered by White law students too. Consequently, students in both focus groups pointed out that this familiarity provided them with a much clearer understanding of what was expected and gave them a clearer idea of what stronger and weaker responses might look like – *and why*. This clarity seemed to directly correspond with reportedly lower levels of exam-related anxiety when doing this type of assessment. It also boosted their confidence in relation to performing well and producing higher quality work, as demonstrated by the following student:

> *I've only ever done the exams. I've never done lab reports and stuff like that, or coursework. My A-Levels, none of it was coursework, it was all*

> *exams. That's all I'm used to. So, doing exams doesn't really stress me out or anything, I feel a lot more confident with them over other things. (Kerry, White Physics Student)*

By the same token, and perhaps rather unsurprisingly, White physics students generally disliked coursework-based assessments. This was mostly because they were seen to be less of an exact science. In turn, the marking process for coursework and lab reports were believed to be dependent on both the content of the answer and the subjective preferences of the individual assessor. Ultimately, they saw coursework as less secure ground for achieving higher-level grade outcomes.

> *Yes, I prefer [exams]. You've got a definitive right or wrong. I just prefer maths to writing out stuff. Because again it is just down to opinion. It's quite ambiguous when people are marking it. It's just down to if they like how you write, your certain style. If they don't like that, they can hold it against you and stuff. But when it comes to physics exams or maths, just with numbers. That's an answer. There's no question about it. (Zoe, White Physics Student)*

> *So say if you're doing a lab report, then there's obviously certain criteria to be met. But I feel like it's slightly more subjective in how it's marked by someone. One person could look at it and think you've written a great report, and then another person could come along and say, actually this isn't quite what I was looking for in a lab report. Purely because one person's opinion of your work could vary from another person's. Whereas if you did a test, an exam, the answer is either right or wrong... (Beth, White Physics Student)*

Presentations as a form of assessment were generally enjoyed by almost all of the White student participants across all disciplines for the following reasons. Biology students claimed that this form of assessment provided them with instant feedback in real time. They also welcomed the added opportunity to show deeper knowledge, typically through the question-and-answer component of the assessment. This was also the case for sociology students who asserted that they particularly enjoyed the synchronous and instant dialogic nature of this type of work. White students in other focus groups also said that they appreciated the fact that in presentations they were able to recover errors and show wider knowledge in their responses to assessors' questions and probes, and in real time.

> *I prefer oral presentations, actually. Because I feel like, when you write something down, that is set in stone. But, when you have an oral presentation, then, if something goes wrong, you can always answer questions from whoever is watching you. Whoever is assessing you. (Triona, White Sociology Student)*

> *Presentations give you good feedback in the sense that I often get told that I'm quick when I'm talking. So I'll have to try and slow myself down for the next ones. (Mel, White Biology Student)*

When it came to dissertations and research projects, in all cases White students were generally the most positive raced group in their views and experiences. This was particularly evident when it came to feeling confident about whether their topic of choice could be supported and supervised by the existing expertise or demographic within their faculties. For the most part, the only concerns voiced were routine anxieties that coalesced around deciding what to do their project on. Or the general challenges of managing a year-long project, while keeping on top of the demands of other modules at the same time.

> *I'm really looking forward to [the dissertation], and especially with the new options of working with a lecturer or a local organisation and things like that. That's really got me excited about thinking, what can I do? My major fear at the moment is timing and just not being able to think of something which is good enough. (Sarah, White Sociology Student)*

Some of the White students in this study illustrated an impressive level of self-awareness when it came to what we might describe as some of the race and class-related advantages that they enjoyed when it came to their experiences of the final year research project. They were, for example, acutely conscious of some of the ways that their raced and classed biographies meant that they could explore almost all and any aspects of their lives in their dissertation in almost all cases. They were also cognisant of how this advantage also applied to their ability to directly relate the majority of their assessment tests, and curriculum content more broadly, to their own lived experiences. Importantly, they claimed that this relatability translated directly into higher grade outcomes. It enabled them to better comprehend content, understand the assignment task, better synthesise an answer or add a critical dimension to their answers. All of this gave them a better chance of securing a higher-grade score.

Some White students were also acutely aware that this experience was not always universal or shared by their friends and peers who were from other raced and classed backgrounds.

> *If you read something, you [can] put your own personal experience in it to make sense of it. (Laura, White Law Student)*

> *I just found a lot of the issues within the topics to be just a lot more interesting [and relatable]. So, it was a lot more easy when it came to revision, to study them. (Kim, White Law Student)*

> *I feel like, because I'm white, middle-class and British, the [assignment] questions are always geared towards me. Whereas I feel like other people might not feel that... (Claire, White Sociology Student)*

EXPERIENCES OF ASSESSMENT SUPPORT

Students across all four focus groups reported inconsistencies in the levels and amount of support and guidance that they had received from module convenors. In some cases, support was described as excellent, but the amount and effectiveness of the support provided largely depended on the individual module convener.

> *I think it's very much based on the lecturer or the module leader. Sometimes, when introducing a new topic, [some have] been amazing. And [when it comes to] a new assessment, they'll explain it completely. (Sarah, White Sociology Student)*

> *Before the exam, [the lecturer] had a specific exam session and [they] went, so, 'this is how many people got firsts. This is how many people got two-ones', etc. 'This is where the majority of people messed up. This is what they did wrong....' But [the lecturer] clearly went over it and said, 'this is where people mess up. This is an example of a good piece of work that I've had over the past few years.' And [they]'d go through that really in detail. And that's my best ever exam to date. (Kelly, White Sociology Student)*

In most instances, students reported receiving very little or unhelpful support in the lead up to undertaking their assessments. White sociology and physics students, for example, felt that they were too often left to learn through trial and error. This meant that when students were confronted with an unfamiliar form of assessment, such as a lab report and coursework, they were often anxious about basic issues such as: How to go about doing the task? What does a good lab report or coursework look like? And: How to achieve higher level grades?

> *We have a vague [idea of what lab reports are]. You must include introduction [and] things like that. But there's not really strict guidelines on what style's preferred. For example, some people write in passive tense and some people write in the other. So, it just depends. (Beth, White Physics Student)*

> *I know that's kind of a bit of a controversial subject inside the physics department itself, [but] a lot of the students want the mark scheme. So they know exactly how to do the questions. But they're [faculty] adamant that they won't give them to us. We get numerical answers. So, some of the questions... if it's like a question where we have to show something, unless it's been covered in lectures or in the recommended textbook, we're kind of a bit stuck. (Mary, White Physics Student)*

> *We did a module... last year, and you have to design a ... poster. And that, none of us knew what we were doing with that. And the lecturer wasn't clear on it either. [The lecturer] wasn't guiding us on what we were meant to do. It was like: 'Oh, just do what you think is best.' And I was like: 'No, I don't know what I'm doing. I'm not a graphic designer, I'm doing sociology!' (Jess, White Sociology Student)*

> *...We're meant to do a blog... but [the lecturer] didn't really say what kind of blog [they]wanted. [First they said they] wanted it to be informative. And then [they] wanted some reference[s]!? (Sarah, White Sociology Student)*

In the main, when students were introduced to assignments that were alien to them, little 'adequate' assessment support was provided. Mary, Jess and Sarah's general point (above) is that this meant students were more-often-than-not expected to instinctively know how to complete their assignments or expected to learn on the job. Students took this to mean that figuring out what to, and what not to do, *seemed to be* what some lecturers thought was part of the learning processes: A position which they disagreed and rejected outright.

In the absence of consistent assessment support that satisfied their learning needs or provided the answers to their questions and confusions about their assessments, the White student cohort had the largest share of students who reported being able to lean on friends, parents, siblings or extended family members who had direct and previous experiences of the academe, for helpful support and guidance. They were also the group who contained the most amount of people who claimed that they would seek out support and assistance from their lecturers if they needed it.

Of course, this experience was not shared by all the White students in our sample. For example, it was especially not the case for most of the participants who were the first in their family (henceforth FIF) to attend university or from what we might describe as working-class households. The following comments from the law and physics students illustrate how for those that did not have access to these cultural resources, 'figuring out' what was required to succeed in their assessments was a long and steep learning curve, which could take as long as three years – or the entirety of their time as undergraduate students.

> *I'm in my third year now. I feel like third year is the first year where I've known what's expected of me. I think partly that's because it's took me three years to fully adapt to the level which is required at university. I think it was quite a big jump going from college to university. (Becky, White Law Student)*

> *I think it took me a long time to really get the knack of what I'm supposed to do and how I'm supposed to do it, and the style of writing . . .. I think it took me three years to understand what that really is, and get the best out of my assessments, to get the best grades possible. (Zoe, White Physics Student)*

Zoe and Becky's accounts illustrate how some students successfully – albeit eventually – work out how to succeed in 'doing' their assessments. However, for the majority of undergraduate students from these backgrounds here (and arguably across the academe), these 'hidden rules of the game' are never fully acquired. Moreover, the repetition of failure that often accompanies learning the rules of particular forms of assessment while 'on the job', often have a direct and negative psychological impact on students' confidence and sense of efficacy for particular forms of assessment in the short, medium and longer term.

Frustrations at the lack of consistent and effective assessment support were compounded by a marking-criteria that students often found to be opaque and difficult to understand. For example, the subjectivity in the criteria for what made a piece of coursework or presentation a 'strong good' (68%) or a weak 'very good' (72%) only added to the suspicions held by many White Science, Technology, Engineering and Mathematics (STEM) and law students that coursework-based assessments were much more prone to interpretation and lecturer bias. This reinforced their preferences for modes of assessment that were determined by much more precise and objective calculations and formula.

> *I think just to add on what Participant Three was saying, when you write a report there's a marking criterion, but it's not standardised ... So, it is just luck of the draw as to whether you get someone marking it that likes your style or not. (Alex, White Physics Student)*

Unhelpful guidance appeared to be something that was equally as frustrating to students as was a lack of consistent guidance. For White sociology students, this included instruction that lacked guidance on the specific assignment task. It also included what we might describe as 'passive' modelling exercises. For example, students spoke of staff making previous examples of 'good' and 'bad' coursework available to them. They were quick to point out that what *made these* essays 'good' or 'bad' was not always obvious by just reading them. Nor had their teachers taught them what it was that made the examples stronger or weaker. Against this, they called for more 'hands on' or active exercises, which made clear what it was that specifically made work successful and how this related to the marking criteria.

> *My module this semester, we had a style of writing [assessment] we never had to experience before. We've never been faced with before. And we got no support as to how to go about writing it. Whereas with*

other forms of assessment ... we got a lot of extra help... But nothing for this ... We were then expected to produce this piece of coursework for [our] assessment without any further help... But they've just thrown you in the deep end and expect you to know how to write like that. (Mel, White Biology Student)

I feel like some modules just prepare you better in a sense that they just have lectures where they go over previous exam papers. (Poppy, White Biology Student)

I think often we get given a rubric or we get a generalised: 'This 82. This is 85, [or] whatever grade.' And the descriptions for them never really fit the exact assignment. They're just very general. And even for a First, you need a sound understanding of something. I don't know what the hell that's meant to mean! A sound understanding of content? [That] can be interpreted in such a different way. And we might think something is a sound understanding but a lecturer will probably disagree with us. (Terresa, White Biology Student)

Some of my lecturers will basically add slides to the end of their lectures where they'll give you some questions or something like ... the main points that you need to know for that lecture. So, I thought a good idea for that would be to incorporate basically that summary slide, those key points that you need to know... And it'd be good if every lecturer could do that because some lecturers do it, some don't, obviously. (Siobhan, White Biology Student)

Against this, White students across all subjects stated that they needed the following support prior to completing their assessments: exercises which clearly illustrated what stronger and weaker assignments looked like and taught them why they were; a 'to do list'; to be briefed on common mistakes; a more interactive and 'hands-on' approach to helping them to understand all aspects of the assessment and marking criteria; consistent guidance across all modules; and summary slides on PowerPoints that signposted the 'need to know information' to help guide revision. They also wanted this guidance for all of their assignments, including those which they had regularly done at school or in college, but not at undergraduate level.

Feedback

How helpful and accessible did White students find processes and practices of feedback? All the students staunchly argued that effective feedback was essential and key to achieving successful grade outcomes. However, like the pre-assessment guidance, their experiences of feedback support were uneven. Written feedback was too often convoluted or phrased in a way that was opaque or jargon heavy. In many cases, it left students unsure of how to improve their work. Another issue for students was that it often highlighted what was lacking in their work, but frequently failed to clearly illustrate how to improve future pieces of work in a way that was user-friendly and clear. Additionally, long texts of feedback often failed to distinguish between what we might describe as more significant grade-determining improvements (such as structure, content, evidence, critical thinking) and stylistic improvements – although these are not mutually exclusive in all cases. Students also wanted clearer feedback for improvement on their assignments, and even for times when they were awarded 60% and above, as the following comments indicate.

> *I got a 2:1 last semester on it. Every point that he'd made on the marking, on the actual work was saying 'this was good'. But then the overall feedback was 'you just didn't explain this one term', and that was it... So, that makes me wonder where the other 30 marks have gone. For me to only get a 2:1, and for him only give me that feedback. So, when I came to do ... another module, this semester, I had nothing to go off of because I got a 2:1 with no feedback. So I don't*

> know how I was meant to improve on something like that. (Poppy, White Biology Student)

> I feel like, when I hand in a good piece of work, then the feedback is useful, because it tells me what I've done well. But, when I hand in a bad piece of work, they just tell me, oh, you haven't done this. They don't tell me how to do it better. So, I feel like, if I didn't do it well, there was a reason, and it was because I didn't know how to do it better. So, if you're telling me this is missing, I know this is missing, I've written this piece of work. But why is it missing? How do I do it? Because, clearly, I wasn't able to do it before, so I wouldn't be able to do it after you're feedback as well, so it's not really useful. (Triona, White Sociology Student)

Issues with clarity in written feedback were argued to be circumvented by face-to-face (oral) feedback. White students were extremely positive about this feedback method. It facilitated a constructive dialogue with lecturers. It was a platform where they felt they could talk more freely about their work and be provided with fuller explanations for the grades they had received. It was also helpful because it was not delivered in the usual academic language that was employed by academics in their written discourse. This more conversational approach helped develop students' understanding of the assessment and provided them with useful and clear guidance on future assessments.

The White STEM students in our sample were particularly positive about the feedback they received through an open-door policy. This was a policy where students were encouraged to see this as space where they could discuss any aspect of their modules and challenge staff on any area of feedback or assessment provision. Clearly, this policy had a positive impact here.

Importantly, the open-door forum was facilitated by a remarkably positive relationship between staff and students. The following accounts from STEM students Alex, Mary, Terresa and Mel capture how White STEM students generally saw their lecturers more as colleagues rather than as teachers. In this forum, students reported feeling supported and had no hesitation in seeking support from their lecturers. Most impressively, they even described this open-door policy as a space where they could challenge grades, offer constructive criticism on the support that they received during the module and where they would not be judged negatively (for doing so).

> *But yes, I know just about every single one of them [her lecturers], and they're all very friendly. So, I don't know if it's the same for every department, but we have an open-door policy. So, we can go and talk to them anytime we want – about pretty much anything. And I think that's probably the best thing. That you build a rapport with any lecturer, and you can ask them for help about any subject. (Alex, White Physics Student)*

> *I feel like, as well, I'm not being judged so much. I'm not worried ... I feel like if I go wrong somewhere ... whoever is assessing them will look at it and feel like they want to help me more. As opposed to, I'm being criticised, if that makes sense... I think, I remember being told in foundation year, to think of lecturers as my colleagues, rather than my superiors. And I completely agree with that frankly. I think if you can see them as being level to you, then it takes away any intimidation that I might have when I'm being assessed as such. (Mary, White Physics Student)*

> *Yes, I find, as well, when you actually have a face to face, sit down tutorial with the person about the assessment it makes such a big difference. We have approached members of staff and been like: 'Well we don't feel like we've got any help for this.' And they are like: 'Oh well we put an example on Blackboard'. Or: 'We've put a guideline on Blackboard, the rubric's up.' (Terresa, White Biology Student)*

> *It's like, well that can be interpreted in so many different ways, it makes such a big difference when you actually sit down and tell them they need to explain it to you face to face. And you can actually ask them questions about it rather than just bombarding them with email after email. (Mel, White Biology Student)*

SOME CONCLUSIONS

Ahmend and Cushing (2021) highlight the extent to which Standard English Tests are informed by the speech patterns of the White British middle-classes. They argue that one consequence of this is that Standard English Tests double as a mechanism which advantage the cultural capitals, currencies and resources of White British middle-class students. Put simply, they sketch out how students whose racialised and classed biographies best align with this construction found themselves accounted for in, and able to successfully navigate, these tests. This underpinned their general academic successes when compared to peers from other race and classed backgrounds.

This point was applicable to the general experience of White student participants in this study in an extant way. The White students' stories of assessment showed that in a general sense, most were able to successfully access all modes of assessment. This did not mean, however, that students did not have preferences for certain forms of assessment or found all areas of the assessment process universally accessible.

With regards to the former, we saw how preferences for specific modes of test were frequently connected to their perceptions of their own innate strengths and learning styles. Or they were the result of a greater familiarity with a type of assessment or a greater trust in the marking process for that type of test. With regards to the latter, for example, we saw how issues accessing pre- and post-assessment support appeared to be rooted in issues relating to class. Students from less affluent households, or who were FIF, found penetrating academic discourse difficult or did not have access to the kinds of social networks that could plug the gaps in support or translate the impenetrable language used in learning outcomes or marking criteria, respectively.

Put simply, scholars such as Moncrieffe (2020) and Ahmed and Cushing (2021) have illustrated the ways in which curricula and assessment in compulsory education often 'works' more advantageously for students who are White. We have seen how this assertion is also applicable for White students in HE, especially in relation to levels of enjoyment and access in a general sense. Obviously, this experience was not blanket or essentialised. The ability to access all areas of assessment in HE was uneven, especially for students from less affluent households.

The extent to which the race(less) and class influenced experiences of assessment described here are directly applicable to students of colour, and specifically to those who self-describe as being Black or Black heritage, is where our attention now turns.

3

BLACK BRITISH STUDENTS' EXPERIENCES OF ASSESSMENT

What are Black British undergraduates' experiences of specific modes of assessment? What are their experiences of support and of being able to access and utilise feedback and feed forward? What are the unifying and diverging experiences of assessment for Black students who are studying different degrees? These three questions shape the parameters of this chapter.

My historical study of generational differences across first-, second- and third-generation Black communities in the British East Midlands illustrated the extent to which the Black experience in social life and leisure in the 21st century are, to varying degrees, both homogenous and heterogenous (Campbell, 2016). For example, in a general sense, all Black communities in the UK continue to experience racialised processes of exclusion. However, this experience is uneven. It is fractured along lines of class, gender, disability and so on. The stories of the Black British students explored in this chapter illustrate how, in higher education spaces, the Black experience in assessment is equally complicated and dynamic.

BLACK STUDENTS' EXPERIENCES OF DIFFERENT TYPES OF ASSESSMENT

Issues of access appeared to be the central factor that determined whether certain forms of assessment were enjoyable or not for the majority of Black students surveyed across all four disciplines. For example, most Black biology and law students showed a preference for exams.

> *I prefer exams. I feel like I'm better at preparing for them. I can have my timetable and I know what I need to do. (Devon, Black Law Student)*

> *I prefer exams over assignments because I feel like with the assignments it's hard to stick to the time … Simply because, as well as trying to complete an assignment, I have other things to do … It's a lot. (Alice, Black Law Student)*

> *You know with my exams, even if I'm a little bit little bit behind, there's that time that I get to just quickly catch up, and then revise for my exams. (Odesha, Black Biology Student)*

Devon, Alice and Odesha's accounts are particularly illustrative of the ways in which Black students' preferences for this form of assessment coalesced around the fact that the examination period was a fixed point and scheduled at the same time in the timetable each semester. This gave them a clearer idea of when to start planning, preparing and revising.

More generally, the accounts also indicate how Black students' preferences for exams were deeply tied into issues of pragmatism. In this case, which assessment types could be most easily worked around the logistical and class-related challenges that were more likely to be features in their wider lives as students who are from Black households in the UK, such as balancing completing assignments with commuting and commitments to supplementary employment (as such, this preference was also echoed by some working-class and FIF White and South Asian students). (see, for example, Douglas Oloyede et al., 2021; Smith, 2018).

Black law students also preferred exams because the difference between what was required in coursework at FE and HE was more significant than it was for exams. Upon entry to HE, they often found themselves unfamiliar with the core expectations of essay writing at the undergraduate level, such as writing 'long' essays that were sometimes in excess of 3,000 words. Other points that were alien included referencing, structure, style and terminology (such as discuss, evaluate, critically assess and so on). All this required a much steeper learning curve than was needed to 'cope' with exams.

> *When you're set essays, they can be more difficult because sometimes the questions they might be, for example, a quote from a case or something. But you might find that a bit more difficult than if it was an exam, because you have to answer that. Whereas in the exam you have more choice. So, I'd say essays can be more difficult in that sense [because] you're limited. (Tre, Black Law Student)*

> *...Essays - I haven't necessarily been used to sitting down, writing down 3,000 words at once, or 2,000 words. Whereas exams, you know okay, you've got an hour to answer this question. It's just instilled in you from secondary school. So, you've got that preparation. (Alice, Black Law Student)*

Another contributor to this group of students' preference for exams was that essays and coursework tasks were seen to be less straightforward and more counterintuitive than exams. In turn, these forms of assessment represented a higher risk and were seen to be a more certain avenue for adverse marks. For example, essay questions were often worded in 'academic' discourse. This type of phrasing required students to deconstruct or 'decipher' what was being asked, first. A combination of their general unfamiliarity with the academe and its 'classed' cultural currencies and discourse meant that successfully completing this task was especially challenging for students from this background. Furthermore, exams usually have a wide(r) selection of optional questions for students to choose to answer. This gave Black students more chance of finding a question that they felt they could deconstruct and make sense of.

Consequently, the majority of Black law students bemoaned that all this meant that when it came to essays, there was a higher chance of them providing an answer that did not respond directly to the question set, and in turn, a higher chance of them receiving a low(er) grade-award. This raises important pedagogical questions around the objective of this type of assessment. Is it to test students' ability to work out essay questions or to enable them to demonstrate knowledge learnt on the module?

Additionally, Black law students saw the grading process for qualitative assignments such as coursework and essays as much more subjective when compared to the ways in which exams results were calculated. This subjectivity was reflected in what they perceived to be a lack of consistency between what was commented on in feedback, and thus interpreted as valuable, by different markers. Shared stories of some markers overlooking spelling mistakes and others flagging – and possibly penalising – these kinds of discrepancies provided them with additional justification for their wariness and belief in the alacrity of bias and foul play in these types of tests. Grade scores for these kinds of assignments were consequently seen to be dependent on the preferences of the individual marker as much as they were on the content. This left little choice for those seeking high scores but to see essays as unsafe ground, especially when compared to exams.

> *I think yes, you can definitely come across some inconsistencies. You might find one tutor is particularly focused on spelling, punctuation and grammar. Whereas another one is more focused on your referencing. Someone might care about how many cases you've put in. I feel like it really depends on what that tutor looks for, and that can impact what grade you're given. (Val', Black Law Student)*

This did not mean that all Black students in our study preferred exams. Black sociology students, for example, largely preferred written coursework and essays over other forms of assessment.

Similarly, to the Black law and biology students discussed above, their preferences were bound up within issues of pragmaticism. They were partly due to a greater familiarity with essay writing in general, and more specifically, to a greater familiarity with what was expected from them to achieve higher-level grade outcomes in this form of assessment. This was largely because coursework had been the most frequent way in which they had been tested during their time at college, which was often and mostly spent studying either social science, humanities or literary-based subjects. Students also pointed to the fact that the process of drafting an essay gave them more room to reflect on the question, and more chances to develop, edit and redraft their work. This was rehearsed by the few biology students that enjoyed this format too. Both argued that it enabled them to produce work that they could be more confident of securing a higher-grade outcome.

> I think [in] terms of why I struggled with exams... I wasn't sure how to actually answer [the] questions properly. I was never really sure what they were actually looking for. (Jenny, Black Sociology Student)

> Essay type [is my favourite], I think. It gives me more time to plan. To structure it well. And to also go through it and re-jiggle bits that I don't like. continues to say. (Destiny, Black Biology Student)

> I like writing essays. I am good at them. And I am quick. So, when we have coursework and they give us only two weeks to do it, that 5,000 words, I am on it. And within three days, I have written [it]. (Femi, Black Biology Student)

By contrast, on the whole, Black sociology students displayed a lower sense of efficacy when it came to exams. This was despite a similarly long history and exposure to this form of testing. Unlike essays, however, exams were viewed as a 'one-shot' form of assessment. In turn, it represented a riskier forum for illustrating subject knowledge and for achieving success (or desired grade scores). Additionally, students argued that they were less clear on what higher-grade exam responses looked like. Lastly, their scepticism was also connected to the fact that historically, many had not performed well in exams during their time at university, or in the past. Below are some examples of comments in this area:

> *I think I enjoy doing assignments. I feel like there's that structure that we're all aware of now because it's obviously been three years of doing it, so there's that comfortability of knowing what you are doing. (Dede, Black Sociology Student)*

> *I prefer normal essay assignments because I feel that it gives me the time to go and do the research that I need to do. It also allows me to take my time when I'm doing it. (Grace, Black Sociology Student)*

> *With exams, it really comes down to you building up to this one moment... (Kelli, Black Sociology Student)*

What then was the Black student experience in dissertations? Against learning in an environment and curricula that provided few opportunities to meaningfully or extensively study about race and its intersections, Black sociology and law students in particular, viewed dissertations as a rare opportunity to explore issues which related directly to their own lived realities and on what they were 'passionate about'. In most cases, participants wanted to explore issues relating to race or ethnicity. They argued that exploring something that was 'close to them' and which they were 'passionate about' made them inclined to read more, study harder and produce higher quality work.

However, dissertations were also a source of high anxiety for students from this minority ethnic group. Pointing to a lack of staff of colour, and to a lack of staff who *they felt were* interested in race (as reflected in a curriculum and faculty that were both overwhelming White), meant they frequently held little hope of finding supervisors who were comfortable, willing or qualified to supervise race-focused dissertations.

Students also felt that it was 'safer' and more advantageous for success, if they chose to do their dissertations on a topic that aligned with their supervisors' own interest (over their own). Again, a lack of an explicitly racially diverse curriculum (that is, a curriculum with few if any modules explicitly centred on race) and an overwhelming Whitened faculty was seen to be a signal which emphatically told Black students to not pick 'race' as their dissertation topic.

Finding a supervisor who was racially, professionally or genuinely interested in their research area was a significant stressor here. It was argued to be central to having a favourable or less favourable experience, and positive grade outcome.

> *I felt a sense of comfort, as well, when I went in to meet my supervisor for the first time and I did see that [they were] Black, basically. That's what I was really scared of... That was a huge fear for me. If it was a White person, I don't feel like they would have understood what I was saying or what I'm trying to get across. But then just as soon as I saw that person was of Black origin, I just felt this sense of relief and that okay yes, maybe I can actually do well in this. (Kelli, Black Sociology Student)*

> *[Doing your dissertation] It definitely is about having a passion about the topic. Even what we were talking about before with whether your supervisor's race influences that. I think it can but it may not in the sense that just as long as that person has that passion. That's just the driving force for success. (Angela, Black Sociology Student)*

> *If I had someone that wasn't of a Black ethnicity, then they wouldn't know what would be considered sensitive in a dissertation, basically. So yes, there was a huge relief when I realised that this person is obviously of a similar race to me, and even comes from the same area that I was brought up in. So, it really helped. (Bernadine, Black Sociology Student)*

> *I feel like, as a dissertation, when you're doing it you need to make sure you're picking something that you're passionate about... A lot of students that aren't enjoying the dissertation, I feel like it's because they've picked something that they're not passionate about. (Paul, Black Sociology Student)*

In general, Black students showed a remarkably high level of awareness of the structural and everyday processes and inequities that shaped their lives as Black people in all social spaces including in education, and specifically here, in relation to securing equitable award outcomes. For example, students called for anonymous marking in all forms of assessment as one way to protect them from negative racial biases and give them more chance of being judged fairly.

Black students appeared to be wary of all assessments where they could be identified, and especially in 'live' presentations. This was not due to low self-confidence or doubt in their own abilities, but to what they saw as the impact of a racialised capital, which shaped the performances expected by predominantly White and middle-class assessors. For example, Black sociology students believed that the grades they received were influenced, and even at times determined, by their ability to successfully embody White middle-class norms and culture. This included their ability to successfully employ or 'switch' language and symbolic codes and (re)present themselves in ways that they described as 'non-typically' Black.

> *[White students] do better [in presentations] because of that... I don't want to say well-spoken or anything like that, but just...it's just like a different kind of vibe... I think it's just about how you're perceived by people in society in general. So, if you're viewed as that stereotypical Black person, you're not going to do as well... (Paul, Black Sociology Student)*

> *I think with the whole handing in your work with just your student number, I think that puts you at an advantage in a sense that you're not limited ... It doesn't matter what colour you are, what gender you are, it's more just*

> *this is your work. And this is how it's going to be marked up. (Joanne, Black Sociology Student)*

Put simply, in assessments where they are visible to assessors, Black students felt that their grades were determined by a combination of the content of their work, the racial biases held by their teachers *and* when it came to presentations, their ability to perform according to White middle-class cultural norms and values. In this way, students were conscious of the myriad ways in which their raced identities and embodied cultural values *might* work against them in educational spaces and outcomes – and visibility in assessments limited their capacity to navigate this reality.

> *[I]t's always been the case where when I've done my GCSEs or my A-levels, my family's always like, make sure you pray that the person marking your work isn't racist. (Derron, Black Sociology Student)*

BLACK STUDENTS' EXPERIENCES OF ASSESSMENT SUPPORT PROCESSES AND PRACTICES PRIOR TO, AND AFTER, COMPLETING ASSIGNMENTS

In general, teaching (best-)practice orthodoxy encourages academics to employ as wide a range of assessments as possible within modules. This is proffered to be beneficial for all learners (see for example Dal Bianco, 2022). However, Black students felt that when confronted with assessments, in some cases they were given little practical and *useful* support and instruction. This was especially the case when introduced to unfamiliar tasks, such as conducting a research project (e.g. writing a literature review, methodology, etc.), blog writing, critical reflections, portfolios and so on.

> *I think last year I was doing [a module] and we had to break it [the assignment] down into a literature review and methodology and things like that. We had never done anything like that before. Yet again, there was that assumption that we should just know what we are*

> doing. Even when I did ask for help, I was confused still. (Viv', Black Sociology Student)

> For that module it literally was assumed that we would know what to write. We didn't know how much we were meant to write and what style we were meant to write in. (Grace, Black Sociology Student)

> A portfolio in one module isn't going to be the same as a portfolio in another module. I feel that's what the issue is, as well, because I could have previously done a portfolio in one module, but the next one is asking me for something different and presenting it differently. So, if I don't know how to do it. Then I'm obviously going to get a bad grade, because, first of all, it's not something I'm used to, and wouldn't know how to structure it. So, providing an example would probably just remove all the issues. (Joanne, Black Sociology Student)

Black law and sociology students explained that the quality of support they received prior to completing their tests was a central and determining factor in their ability to perform well, and praised instances where they had received helpful support. They particularly welcomed preparatory hand-outs, detailed guidance materials and workshops around specific assessments. In most instances, however, there were glaring inconsistencies in the levels and types of support offered when it came to different types of assessment and in the support offered in different modules.

> I feel like it was only this year when other lecturers ... actually showed us what a first-class essay looks like. Just things like that is helpful because let's say in secondary school A-level, you're provided with mark schemes throughout the year. You're provided with what an A-grade essay is meant to look like. So, just with that it actually shows you, okay this is what I'm not doing. This is what I need to do. We don't have

> that. It's almost like you're just left in the dark. (Bernadine, Black Sociology Student)

> One particular person from first year that I would say that really does go above and beyond. Not only are the handouts amazing, but they have… these sessions where you can just drop in and speak about their topic, their subject area and you can ask them anything about it. And that went all the way from September, right up to our exams. (Val', Black Law Student)

On the whole, participants welcomed variety in their assessment options. But variation alone was not key to helping them succeed. Instead, they asserted that *more* structured and *consistent* preparatory support and guidance for all assessment types across all modules would be more beneficial for ensuring success, especially during their transitions from FE to HE. Interestingly, students also wanted more structured support for modes of assessment that they had done in FE or at any undergraduate level, where the expectations for success had changed (such as, being taught the different expectations between what is required in a 2.1 essay at level 1 and a 2.1 essay at level 2). In most cases, however, the variety of assessment options made available, as well as the standard and amount of support they (did or did not) received was largely dependent on the individual lecturer.

> I do think some [modules] they do give more help. But I don't know if that's just based on different lecturers just deciding to go more in depth and have more sessions for particular assessment and coursework. (Marcus, Black Biology Student)

> I haven't written a long piece of writing. Which, obviously, it's different. I understand. Because it's Biology. There's less storytelling, if you like. But Psychology and English were more long kind of pros that I had to write. So, it's a bit different. It's difficult for me to adjust. (Femi, Black Biology Student)

> *If I feel like there is no support from the actual module conveners, or there's no effort to have little support groups, or something, in the run up to exams. (Tasha, Black Biology Student)*

> *There are special ways to write it that you would have been taught ... But for people who may not have been here, or who may have come to England for uni, they would not know that. Because they wouldn't have been taught that in their English wherever else they came from. So, it's a barrier for them. (Destiny, Black Biology Student)*

Where pre-assessment support was available, it too often focused on preparing students for a test, rather than focusing on how to 'do' it – that is, how to construct higher-scoring responses. For example, one Black participant noted how their mock exams helped them get used to writing under timed conditions but provided little help or insight into how to actually construct a higher-grade answer, or for what types of knowledge they were being tested on (content, argument, criticality, rote and so on). Put simply, students argued that this type of assessment coaching was redundant, even pointless, if it did not also explicitly include teaching them what was required to be successful.

What were Black students' experiences of feedback? When it came to the support and guidance that students received after their assessments had been completed, written feedback was claimed to often be vague and not precise enough to provide meaningful guidance.

> *With coursework, when we get our marks back we have little side comments. So, it's 'oh you could have done this better'. They're still not explaining to us like how... (Tasha, Black Biology Student)*

> *I don't feel that it's very clear. Because on the mark schemes the words are so generic ... You have 'good', 'very good' and 'great'. But it's like where is that*

> *distinction? It's subjective, really and truly. (Destiny, Black Sociology Student)*
>
> *The feedback literally would just be like, 'good, poor, explain, not detailed, scanty.' One word. What does that mean? What is that? (Tre, Black Law Student)*
>
> *So, you might get comments like: 'Okay, this sentence doesn't make sense.' All right, but can you tell me how I can make it better? What do I need to do to make it better? (Alice, Black Law Student)*

Students' frustrations were clearly linked to a perception of the feedback process as something which was subjective and not clearly linked to grading criteria in any meaningful or understandable way. It was clear that the majority of participants were equally concerned with what they had done wrong, as well as with what they had to do for improvement, and importantly, with being *shown what* 'improvement' looked like.

The key takeaway here is that in the Black student experience, written feedback was seen as a reactive learning tool instead of a proactive mechanism for change and improvement in future. A general inability to access the kinds of social networks that were advantageous for navigating HE meant that to access the key information required for success, either prior to completing their work or after their work had been graded, required students to reach out to staff. However, this was not straightforward. Almost all Black student participants from across all disciplines explained that they seldom felt comfortable or safe approaching staff to either unpack or explain the written feedback that they had provided them.

SOME CONCLUSIONS

The chapter has illustrated how processes of anti-Black exclusions in assessment are direct, subtle and complex. They are the outcome of wider structural processes, such as a lack of a representative faculty or expertise to provide academic support or supervision in race, and a White and Eurocentric faculty which can stymie the engagement of Black students. They also include the ways in which assessments, related practice and expectations prioritise the currencies that are unevenly clustered within White middle-class communities.

Rollock (2022) asserts that Black British citizens exhibit remarkable levels of agency to navigate and survive racially hostile spaces in their everyday lives – which include pretty much all social and employment spaces that they inhabit in the UK. The accounts here add weight to this observation. The accounts shared by the Black undergraduates from law, sociology, physics and biology highlight how they nimbly navigate racially exclusive processes and barriers in assessment when in higher education – although, their testimonies also show us that they may not always be conscious of when and how they enact these forms of resistance. For example, in most cases, students preferred and consciously gravitated to assessments that fitted their lives, which as people from Black and working-class households required them to strategically opt for assessments that fitted around travelling and work commitments. They also preferred assessments where they could not be identified, because anonymity shielded them from the threat of negative teacher biases and a White gaze which positioned them as educationally deviant, culturally. Their 'toolkit' for surviving assessment also included giving a physical and verbal performance that distanced themselves culturally from their Blackness and aligned with White cultural norms when in presentations. In doing so, their accounts reveal something telling. It illustrates how anti-Black racism in assessment can be both a psychological and embodied experience. It is a violence that quite literally bares on the minds and the bodies of Black students when in the academe.

4

BRITISH SOUTH ASIAN STUDENTS' EXPERIENCES OF ASSESSMENT

In a general sense, the history of inclusion for the diverse populations that constitute the British South Asian community in the 8 decades that have followed World War 2 is complex, uneven and heterogenous. During this period, they have all experienced structural, systemic, overt and covert forms of racial discriminations and microaggressions in all areas of social life. However, these exclusions have been experienced in various and uneven ways.

The Indian heritage British citizens that were predominantly of the Hindu faith who relocated to the UK via East Africa during the 1960s and 1970s, for example, brought with them various social and cultural currencies and business acumen (Herbert, 2007). This capital softened some of the negative effects of many of the structural racisms that were being experienced more acutely by other British South Asian citizens in employment and housing. It also paved the way for a swifter ascension into the British middle- and political-classes for members from this group, than has so far been experienced by some of the other South Asian communities who relocated more directly from India, Pakistan or Bangladesh or those who are of other faiths (Saini, 2023). Additionally, South Asian Britons from these other faith groups or ethnic communities also continue to experience much more acute forms of structural racism in employment, health and wealth as well as routinely face more overt forms of anti-religious discriminations at all levels of social life in the UK, including in compulsory education (Saini, 2022. see also Archer & Francis, 2007).

Archer and Francis (2007) point to differences in the way in which British South Asian students from different faith backgrounds are often framed by their teachers in compulsory education spaces in the 21st century. They assert that young British people of the Sikh or Hindu faith are routinely considered to be culturally passive and studious and consequently, framed as 'ideal immigrants' and seen as 'achievers'. In turn, they argue that they generally have a relatively positive experience *in* British classrooms. This is contrasted with the 'believers' label, which is often used to denote British South Asian students of the Islamic faith, who are routinely and conversely framed as aggressive, problematic and culturally incompatible with 'liberal' Western value systems. In turn, they experience much higher rates of exclusion, surveillance and lower expectations and grade outcomes.

While such extreme frames and starkly contrasting experiences were not so obviously visible in the accounts of the British South Asian undergraduate students discussed below, there were noticeable commonalities and contrasts along the axis of diaspora and religion within their own stories of assessment in the academe.

BRITISH SOUTH ASIAN STUDENTS' EXPERIENCES IN, AND OF, DIFFERENT TYPES OF ASSESSMENT

On the whole, most of the British South Asian student participants across all of our focus groups reported enjoying all forms of assessment. In most cases, preferences appeared to be rooted in issues of pedagogy. For others, their preferences were deeply connected to the structural issues that are faced by racialised minorities in higher education and in social life more widely in contemporary Britain. For students of the Islamic faith, for example, preferences for assessments were determined by which ones they felt they were less likely to face anti-religious biases.

Most of the British South Asian biology students in our survey preferred exams. This was because they were a continuation of the types of assessment that they undertook during their time in further education. Sitting exams was described as a relatively short and therefore less painful experience. Interestingly, this was not about particular modes of assessment but about where they felt they had the best chance of providing high quality answers. For example, the few South Asian Biology students who enjoyed essays similarly pointed to liking this mode of assessment because it gave them the time and space to formulate, edit and develop their answers and produce more expansive answers.

> *I personally prefer exams because it's for one day. You only have to revise for that one exam. It's not like an essay where it's continuous, so it's out of the way. As soon as you've done the exam it's out of the way, I guess. (Inderpal, South Asian Biology Student)*

> *[I]n essays, I can go back and forth. If I'm not feeling well on one day, then on the next day I can sit for a longer time and try and work through. (Saeedah, South Asian Biology Student)*

The South Asian physics student focus group reported that open book exams were their preferred mode of assessment, because having the text to hand provided them with the necessary 'support' to better conceptualise and apply theory and, in turn, to produce higher-quality answers.

This was preferred over other modes of assessment, such as essays and coursework, which were said to be a more alien form of testing to them. They asserted that because there was a general lack of clear guidance provided by staff on issues such as how to structure and successfully 'do' these types of assessments, this meant they often had to rely on previous experiences and knowledge to succeed. Given this situation, it is unsurprising that they opted for exams. Put simply, they did not prefer exams because of any intrinsic reasons, but because they felt that, in most cases, neither their previous educational experiences nor the assignment support offered in HE had prepared them to 'do well' in the multiple and alternative ways in which they were now assessed in the academe.

Assessments where students' identities were visible, such as presentations, were problematic and cause for high anxiety for some South Asian students. Students who described themselves as being of the Islamic faith felt that this 'visibility' left them open to ethnic and religious anti-education stereotypes and biases, which impacted negatively on the grade scores that they were awarded. Suspicions of ill treatment, especially of Muslim students, were subscribed to by *all* the South Asian students in our focus groups, and stories of Islamophobic discriminations were corroborated by the accounts of South Asian students who were not of the Islamic faith:

> *They have a very Muslim name. But with them they've actually had multiple experiences where they feel like their mark has been a bit unfair. Especially because we literally do the work together, and the stuff that we come up with is very similar and our ideas are all the same. So surely if what we're coming up with is the same [answer], there shouldn't be a big 30% difference. (Ranju, British South Asian Biology Student who was not of the Islamic faith)*

ISSUES WITH ACCESSING THE ASSESSMENT SUPPORT THAT WAS PROVIDED PRIOR TO COMPLETING THEIR ASSIGNMENTS

Similarly, to the accounts from students from the other raced backgrounds in our survey, British South Asian participants proffered that their ability to gain higher-grade outcomes would be improved with more consistent and expansive pre-assessment support for all forms of examinations. However, this was currently not the case. The following accounts provide some examples of both the helpful and less helpful assessment support that they received.

> *They don't really tell us much on what a weak and strong one [assignment] looks like. They don't give us any examples on, this is a strong answer, this is a weaker answer. So, in terms of that, we don't get any [support]. (Momtaz, South Asian Biology Student)*

> *This last January we had exams, and they didn't really provide mocks or a sample assessment for that exam, and the excuse was that they wanted us to learn how to think rather than learn the answers from past papers, or the sample paper. But I disagree with their reasoning for it, and I think it would have been better to have a sample paper ... [I] can only really think of one [lecturer] that provides this [support of this kind]. (Tara, South Asian Biology Student)*

Against this uneven picture of preparatory support, students called for more standardisation in the support they received. However, this was not a call for more generic support. They wanted module and assignment specific guidance and support that focused on making clear what was required in higher grade answers.

As indicated above, preferences and aversions to assessment types, such as essays and coursework, appeared to stem from a lack of familiarity with these 'new' modes of examination. It also derived from a lack of consistency in the assessment support that they received in preparation for their test. In turn, students called for more guidance which modelled how to do new assessments and, importantly, guidance that provided clear instruction on how to do the tests *well*.

> *It would really help to see examples. Then we [would] know what they actually expect from us. Because we haven't done coursework before, because we have done A-levels. So, we don't have any idea of what they expect from us. So, if we see examples, we get an idea of what they expect from us. (Amardeep, South Asian Physics Student)*

In the absence of a clear understanding of what stronger pieces of work 'look like', or what constitutes stronger and weaker coursework and essay responses, students from South Asian Indian backgrounds, in particular, generally speculated this to mean that these types of assessment were a less exact science and assessed according to more subjective marking criteria. They argued that assessment outcomes here were, most likely, to be influenced by the individual preferences of the assessor. In turn, coursework represented a less secure method for securing higher grades than exams.

> *I feel like it depends on the person marking it. Like what someone might find it to be really good, and someone else might think it's not good at all. (Inderjeet, South Asian Physics Student)*

The South Asian students in this sample argued that pre-assessment guidance was especially important to them. They explained that this was because many of them were the first in their own families to go to university. As such, they did not have family members and social networks that consisted of people who could plug the gaps in their knowledge around assessment, or provide alternative pre-assessment support in the absence of sufficient guidance from their lecturers. While we must be careful of over-generalising, the accounts here corroborate with a wider consensus that a higher percentage of students from South Asian households are still the first to enter HE, when compared to their White peers, and thus, less likely to have access to the same kinds of social and cultural resources that enable their White and middle class peers to more successfully navigate assessment, and HE more widely (Douglas Oloyede et al., 2021).

> *Some of the (South Asian) students they don't really have that support at home because their parents have never done a degree before. So, it's really helpful to get that support from the lecturers. Otherwise, where else can we get that support from? (Raman, South Asian Physics Student)*

BRITISH SOUTH ASIAN STUDENTS' EXPERIENCES OF FEEDBACK AND FEED FORWARD

The importance of feedback (written and oral) was rehearsed among British South Asian students in all of the focus groups. It was seen to be an essential tool that impacted their assessment performance and development. Students described useful written feedback as thorough but concise, with clear signposts to what they had done wrong. It also provided them with instructions on how to improve that specific piece of work and how this advice related to future work.

In most instances, however, South Asian students felt that written feedback was unclear and unhelpful. Moreover, the language used was too often difficult to penetrate, for some. Consequently, it provided little help for enabling them to comprehend why they received a particular grade score, and how to improve in future (and what that improvement look like).

> [S]ome feedback is just telling me the answers right or wrong sort of thing, but then there's some which are actually quite good. (Mumtaz, South Asian Biology Student)

> Sometimes the feedback is very specific to that assessment, so you can't really use it for another assessment. (Raj, South Asian Biology Student)

> [The marker might say:] 'I need to be more concise' But they don't really specify... like which way? If it was like the whole essay? Or just parts of it? (Puja, South Asian Biology Student)

> Good feedback would be telling me what exactly I've done wrong. Not exact. You can say that you've added extra information in the introduction, or they can say that your sentencing wasn't accurate, or grammatical errors. Stuff like that. (Tori, South Asian Biology Student)

> When they are marking us, they tell us that 'this is strong', 'this is weak'. But it's not justified. They're not writing what is good and what is bad. They just say, 'this is bad', and 'this is good'. But why is it good? Why is it bad? Also, they don't tell us how exactly they're marking us. Where did I lose my marks? In that whole essay, it's a 2,000-word essay, how am I

supposed to know where I lost my marks? (Tushee, South Asian Biology Student)

Against these experiences of unhelpful or impenetrable written feedback, interviewees agreed that oral feedback was an essential and alternative platform to gain this knowledge and improve assessment performance. Specifically, they recognised this as a key platform which unpacked many of the assignment issues raised so far, and essential for breaking down and making sense of (written) feedback and feed forward instructions.

They knew that in many ways oral feedback was their only chance of getting this key information for success. However, it was apparent that *accessing* oral feedback was not always a straightforward process *for all South Asian heritage students*. For example, while Science, Technology, Engineering and Mathematics (STEM)-based South Asian students had unlimited access to staff via an open-door policy, their stories indicated that, in practice, oral feedback was not viewed as a safe or secure forum. Students remarked that they often did not feel 'safe' or 'confident' in approaching staff or see 'open-doors' as a forum to participate in open dialogue, where they could ask questions freely without feeling that judgements might be made about their intelligence (or lack of) by their lecturers.

It [would be] nice to talk to them [lecturers] about it, but I'd feel scared to ask them. (Amardeep, South Asian Physics Student)

The lecturers that I know I talk to. But some of the other ones, I maybe hesitate. I don't know... Just scared to ask to ask, really... [They would] probably think I am silly. (Bal, South Asian Physics Student)

SOME CONCLUSIONS

This final descriptive chapter has centred the South Asian student voice and provided a thick description of students from these communities' experiences of assessment. It illustrates how experiences were contrasted along subject lines but also how they were complicated by religion too. These differences were manifest in contrasting perceptions of, and experiences in, different forms of assessment and related processes.

However, we are left with the following important questions which have yet to be answered explicitly: What has mapping the assessment experiences of White, Black and South Asian students on four different undergraduate degrees told us about how the practices and processes of assessment contribute to differences in award outcomes between students of colour and White peers? What does this tell us about why certain heritage students appear to have differing and uneven experiences of inclusion in certain forms of assessment over others? Or better inform us about the extent to which issues of accessibility and inclusion in assessment for minority ethnic students are intrinsic to specific assessment types or connected to wider pedagogical practice? Or tell us about the ways in which wider social and cultural factors – and proxies for race – such as socio-economic background, cultural capital, location and so on, intersect, influence and may contribute to uneven experiences (and in turn performances) of students from specific minority ethnic in particular forms of assessment? These are addressed in the following chapter.

5

CONCEPTUALISING INTER- AND INTRA- RACE-BASED BARRIERS IN ASSESSMENT

What were the unifying and diverging experiences of assessment between Black, South Asian and White students on four different undergraduate degrees? What do these experiences tell us about the ways in which existing assessment and related practices and processes contribute to differences in award outcomes?

SOME OF THE MORE 'OBVIOUS' BARRIERS TO INCLUSION IN ASSESSMENT FOR RACIALISED UNDERGRADUATE STUDENTS

Students' testimonies illustrated some of the more direct ways that their racialised biographies and experiences as people of colour worked against them in assessment processes and directly influenced award outcomes. For example, White students proffered that in most cases they were able to easily relate curriculum, assessments and assessment questions to their own realities and life experiences. This was said to improve their ability to revise, comprehend and conceptualise new theories and for ideas to 'stick'. It was also claimed that in most instances, it enabled them to work out a question's meaning more easily or enabled them to use their own life experiences to better synthesise or add a critical dimension to their answers – and in turn, produce higher quality responses.

The lack of a sufficiently inclusive or decolonised curricula (and faculty) meant that the reverse was true when it came to the experience of students of colour. For example, it was often difficult for Black students to be able to connect content and assessments directly to their own lived realities. It was argued that to do so would facilitate more interest in study and foster a deeper understanding and synthesis. In this way, racially minoritised students are multiply disadvantaged, when compared to White students. They have to work harder than their peers to connect with both assessment *and* curriculum content. It should also be noted that the disadvantage for students of colour – and advantage for White – students in this regard was remarked upon by both White and global majority students. This point was neatly summed by White sociology student, Claire, who stated as fact: 'I feel like, because I'm White, middle-class and British, the (assignment) questions are *always* geared towards me'.

Claire's marked point that it was a combination of her White and middle-class biography that facilitated her advantage reminds us of the need to avoid essentialist notions of race. That such barriers are to some degree experienced by all students from socio-economically challenged backgrounds. By the same token, the intersected nature of these race *and* class-based barriers in assessment mean that they can only be partially navigated by students of colour from middle-class households (see Wallace, 2017).

Students' stories also showed us how some assessments are experienced differently along the axis of race and faith. British Black students and British South Asian students who were visibly of the Islamic faith, for example, both asserted that being 'visible' to assessors left them particularly vulnerable to unequal treatment *because* of their raced backgrounds. When discussing their experiences of presentations, none of the White student participants pointed to having to navigate issues which directly related to their race. By contrast, South-Asian students of the Islamic faith argued that visibility left them open to anti-Islamic biases from their assessors and resulted in lower grade outcomes. Interestingly, a number of the non-Muslim South-Asian heritage participants in the study vouched that, although they felt that *they* were not subject to these specific forms of anti-Islamic discriminations themselves, they were certain that their South-Asian Muslim heritage peers were.

Black student participants on the other hand felt that during 'live' presentations, they had to embody White cultural norms and successfully play them back to assessors to be marked positively. By the same token, they were conscious of the need to avoid giving a performance that could be read or 'viewed' as being *culturally* 'too Black' by examiners (King, 2004). Their testimonies indicated that Black students were conscious that they were assessed in relation to their content, subject knowledge *and importantly* on their ability to successfully embody a specific White and classed performance. This included a verbal, symbolic and bodily performance. Their conscious attempts to provide a rendition of Whiteness to be successful in their assignments demonstrate how students of colour are often acutely aware of how their race and embodied ethnic culture and cultural practices frequently work against them in education spaces, or signals them as educationally sub-normal to assessors, *if not masked* (Wallace & Joseph-Salisbury, 2021).

Such accounts remind us of the heterogeneity of experiences that can exist within and across singular raced and ethnic minority groups in Britain. They also underscore the existence of pervasive anti-Black barriers within HE which the *Race Equality Charter Review: Final Report* in 2021 (Douglas Oloyede et al., 2021), found to characterise the experiences of Black people at all levels of the academe.

Lastly, the disclosures also point to less obvious issues brought about by what students described as a distinct lack of assessment transparency in the marking criteria (discussed below), which impact unevenly on students from different raced backgrounds. This absence facilitated a space for speculation among student participants, especially when their grade scores did not correlate with the effort that they had invested into their assignments, or with 'higher' grade awards given to others who they felt had produced similar standards of work.

It is in the students' speculated explanations where another significant split along lines of race and religion manifests. For example, when such anomalies occurred, White and non-Muslim

South Asian students were more likely to explain these away, as being the result of the inexactness and subjectivity that came with certain forms of qualitative assessment, such as coursework. By contrast, for British Black students and British South-Asian students of the Islamic faith, anomalies in grade outcomes were understood as simply being another example of the inequalities that they had to endure in a UK education system and in a British society, which is routinely and systematically hostile to them. This point was captured when Derron, a Black student, explained: '[I]t's always been the case where when I've done my GCSEs or my A-levels, my family's always like, make sure you pray that the person marking your work isn't racist'.

This points to how a lack of assessment transparency contributes to a psychological violence that is experienced daily by many students of colour in HEPs. The failure of course programmes and module convenors to effectively familiarise students with how work is assessed leaves assessment practices open to these kinds of speculations and psychological traumas, especially by students who are rightly wary and used to be being mistreated because of their race and ethnic identities in late modern Britain.

RACE AND PRE-ASSESSMENT SUPPORT

Student participants across all 12 focus groups viewed what I define as the pre-assessment support (PrAS) that they received prior to and in preparation for their assessments as crucial to their chances of 'success' in assignments. The vast majority, however, bemoaned too often receiving what they described as 'inconsistent' and thus, ineffective support across courses and modules. In almost all of the accounts, the level and quality of PrAS provided were said to 'depend' greatly on the individual lecturer.

For most, PrAS took the form of either being given access to repositories which contained previous graded assignments or being 'taught' assessment skills via training exercises in stand-alone 'study skills' modules, usually during their first year of undergraduate study. In practice, however, these modes of support often proved to be problematic and limited in their efficacy for improving students' assessment literacy. In the case of the latter, for example, students found transferring decontextualised assessment skills learnt on one module, to themed (subject or theory) assignments in another, extremely difficult. It required high levels of 'synthesis', which is a particularly prized and high-level skill in the academe.

With regards to the former, participants explained that simply having access to previously graded assessments showcased to them what assignments at different levels might look like, but seldom explained to them *why* these assignments had scored 'well' or 'poorly'. Nor did they make visible what the criteria for success outlined in the grading criteria 'looked like' or what constituted them in the pieces of work made available to them. This sense of frustration was captured by one Black student who bemoaned: 'We don't know what makes them [previous assignments] good'. In response, participants called for what I describe as 'active' modelling. For the purpose of this book, I loosely define these as activities which provide module specific and 'hands on' assessment support exercises, which teach what it is that makes work successful and how this relates to the marking criteria.

The level of assessment literacy with which students commence undergraduate study is in large part a product of their socioeconomic background and related habitus more than a reflection of their talent. Consequently, scholars such as Channock (2000) have argued that HEPs need to do more to deconstruct the often class-coded academic discourses that shape, cloud and make assessments opaque for a significant number of students who are often described as coming from 'non-traditional' backgrounds, who constitute much of the student body today. Channock's conclusion offers a useful reminder of the power imbalances that exist between academics and especially working-class students in a more general sense. The data here, however, indicates that education processes around assessment within HEPs *intensify and amplify these social and class-related barriers* for many students of colour, whose marginalisation in UK HEPs are experienced through the intersections *of both* race and class (as well as gender, ableism and so on) (see, for example, Meer & Chapman, 2015).

Student participants from minority-ethnic backgrounds' experiences of assessment and related processes empirically illustrate how race and ethnicity *are often proxies for wider conditions of social life,* which often place students from these backgrounds at a disadvantage in HEP curricula and related systems. In this case, for example, systemic and structural inequalities which characterise the current and historical experiences of many people of colour in Britain, means that participants from British South Asian Pakistani and Bangladeshi and Black African and African Caribbean households in particular, remain statistically more likely to live in socio-economically challenged areas. This also means that students from these race and classed backgrounds are also more likely to be the first in their families to go to university, when compared to White peers (Wallace & Joseph-Salisbury, 2021).

Participants in our study from these communities were particularly attuned to these related and legacy race and class-based disadvantages. In turn, they were keen to press the importance of the need for this support for students *like them.* These were students of colour who, according to the participants from global majority backgrounds, were less likely to have access to kin or social networks that were familiar with HE assessment processes and literacy, who could plug any lack of PrAS provided in their modules.

POST-ASSESSMENT SUPPORT AND RACIALISED HABITUS

When I refer to post-assessment support, in a crude sense we are discussing the processes of assessment feedback that inform the students of how the grade score was derived, the things they did well, how to improve on that particular piece of work, and how to improve their assessment practice more generally and going forward.

The students' experiences of feedback across Chapters 2, 3 and 4 illustrated how the effectiveness of oral feedback as a racially inclusive mode of post-assessment support appeared to be predicated on the historical legacies that have shaped the minority ethnic community experience from which the student is connected. In turn, the ability to successfully and fully access and utilise this mode of feedback in particular, as a platform for an equitable two-way dialogue between student and lecturer, was often a performance of racialised advantage, entitlement and a *racialised* habitus.

The previous three chapters illustrated a general consensus among all student participants that they often found *written* feedback to be ambiguous, vague and unclear. Moreover, the language used in this type of dialogue was frequently couched in jargon and specialist terminology, which often made it difficult for some to penetrate. Moreover, almost all of the students from across all three raced backgrounds and subject disciplines argued that it provided little help in enabling them to comprehend why their assignments had received a particular grade score or *how* to improve (and what that improvement looked like).

Issues with written feedback were said to be circumvented by face-to-face or oral feedback. Conversely, this was described as a more helpful platform for students to engage in constructive dialogue with lecturers about their work and provided clear explanations for their received grades. It was also seen to be a key resource that developed their understanding of assessment and related processes. It provided them with useful guidance for future work. Unlike their shared experiences and views of written feedback, however, oral feedback was experienced very differently by the students of colour in our sample, when compared to their White peers.

The science-based programmes that participants were on provided oral feedback via an 'open-door policy'. Here, students were encouraged to freely engage with staff on any issue that they wanted, usually assignment related, at a time that suited them. This forum proved extremely popular among White student participants and appeared to be predicated on remarkably positive relationships between them and the faculty. This was summed up by one White Physics student who explained that she saw her lecturers more as 'colleagues' rather than as teachers. They were also keen to point out that in this space, they had no hesitation in seeking support from their lecturers. They went so far as to describe it as a space where they could challenge the grades they had received, and even offer their lecturers constructive criticism on the support that they had been provided during the module – and not be judged negatively for doing so.

Conversely, oral feedback via this platform was not viewed as a safe or secure forum for South Asian participants, who did not express the same levels of confidence in approaching their lecturers. Nor did they see it as a forum to participate in open dialogue, where they could ask questions freely without feeling that judgements might be made about their intelligence (or lack of) by their lecturers.

The use of one-to-one oral feedback typically via platforms such as open-door policies or open-office hours is encouraged by HEPs. They are often lionised by education practitioners and some decolonising curricula champions for their proclivity for inclusivity and as best practice. For example, in a keynote lecture at University College London in 2021, Jason Arday described this as a channel through which students can engage staff on more equal grounds. Testimonies here, however, demonstrate how this method of post-assessment support approach can be experienced very differently and unevenly by students of colour when compared to White peers. They also provide illustrative examples of how the possession and operation of different forms of racialised habitus often translate into forms of access and exclusion within higher education spaces.

Singh's (2021, p. 5) assertion that a person's racialised habitus 'is a historically formed process of social orientation which constructs within the [racialised] individual a sense of their "place" in any given situation or setting' is useful in enabling us to make sense of the differing narratives of post-assessment support between students of colour and their White peers presented in Chapters 2, 3 and 4. Bourdieu (1990, pp. 98–99) posited that habitus endowed dispositions are formed through access, or restricted access, to certain areas of social life or 'conditions of existence'. He argues that one's habitus seeks to reorganise or circumvent historically oppressive social restrictions by creating a mode of consciousness within the group or individual which self excludes from spaces which have been historically hostile to them – a mode of social self-preservation (Bourdieu, 1990. See also Wallace, 2017).

By extending Bourdieu's concept to account for the intersection of race *and* class, Singh (2021, p. 5) enables us to frame the British South Asian student participants' reluctance to seek oral feedback when compared to their White peers as a (sub)conscious choice, resistance and form of empowerment that has taken place in response to a space which has historically proven to be hostile for, and disinterested in, people like them. Thus, for them, their racial habitus is a 'colonial history' and experience 'turned into nature' (Singh, 2021). As Singh concludes, in 'White colonial spaces such as education, one's [racialised] habitus can lead people [of colour] to exclude themselves from activities such as questioning [W]hite authority' (Singh, 2021, p. 9).

SOME CONCLUSIONS

The lived accounts of students presented in the previous three chapters add to the canon of empirical anti-racism work in education by providing empirical data that illustrates how institutional and cultural processes, which advantage and disadvantage students from different minority ethnic backgrounds, are deeply imbedded within HE assessment (Bhopal, 2018; Wright, 1992). Crucially, this chapter has sketched out some of the nuanced ways in which these processes work to prioritise and marginalise specific race and social capitals, currencies and cultural tools, which are clustered unevenly in certain communities. In doing so, we have seen how assessment and related practices are not 'objective' activities and processes, but cultural and colonial products. They are not neutral, but instead apparatuses, which are influenced and imbued with many of the systems, practices, hegemonies and colonial legacies that have the potential to marginalise, or be experienced unevenly by, students of colour. Most current assessment and related practices play a crucial role in maintaining the existing racial and class status quo that characterises the academe in the UK.

An inductive methodological approach helped me to frame three emergent sites of racial discrimination and violence within HE assessment: in pre-assessment support, post-assessment support and in relation to direct forms of racial inequity in assessment. For example, a lack of standardised and 'active' PrAS activities and policies across taught undergraduate modules, often left student participants with two options: to 'learn how to do' assessments successfully through a costly process of trial and error; or to rely on wider kin- and social-networks for support. However, it was also clear that wider historical and social systemic and structural processes of marginalisation, that have characterised the Black and minority ethnic experience in the UK for over a century (see Campbell, 2016), meant that the latter channel for support was more readily available to students from White *and* affluent households and less so to those from minority ethnic and working-class backgrounds.

Minority ethnic student calls for active PrAS were also indicative of different pedagogical positions embraced in HEPs compared to comprehensive or state education, which has embraced more *Assessment For Learning* (AFL)-based learning principles. The basic tenet of AFL-type models of learning is that for a student to produce higher-level work they must first know – or be shown – what it looks like. This pedagogical practice is at times juxtaposed to many of the cultural practices within HEPs more generally, which sometimes view attempts to standardise practice and provide assessment 'modelling' as something which stifles talent, innovation and excellence, instead of supporting, nurturing and facilitating it.

State education is also the educational route that domicile global majority students are most likely to have come through prior to arriving in HE (see Wallace & Joseph-Salisbury, 2021). It is important to note that the AFL frame can also be read as an educational response to a 'deficit model' philosophy (Fulcher, 2021); that is, to frame students as vessels that need to be adjusted, fixed and implanted with the 'right' knowledge, capital and currency to be successful in UK HEPs (Bryne et al., 2020). To be clear, I do *not* subscribe to this philosophical viewpoint. Instead, I sought to (re)centre our critical gaze on to the cultures, pedagogies, processes, structures, policies, and sub-cultural practices within HEP assessment (Bhopal, 2018; Richardson, 2015), in an attempt to illustrate, empirically, the need to evolve them to account more fully for the varied realities of all the students that constitute student bodies in HE in late modern Britain. In doing so, this discussion adds to the body of work which seeks to shift the pedagogical focus away from *how we make students ready* for HE, to *how we make the academe ready* for the full range of students we serve today and in future (Hockings, 2010).

With regard to the student experiences of post-assessment support, we saw how the effectiveness of oral feedback via open-door or open spaces as a platform for meaningful and two-way critical dialogue depend greatly on which students have historically been welcomed in HE and thus, who feel safe and entitled to engage in this dialogue with their lecturers. It illustrates the extent to which oral feedback and 'open-door' policies are spaces of Black and minority ethnic inequity, and require much more reflexivity than currently given if they are to work equitably for all students. Put another way, while universities often celebrate feedback via open-door and/or open-space policies, student testimonies remind us that *who* feels – and is allowed to feel – able to enter into that space and dialogue in a more equal way, requires more than educators simply leaving their doors 'open'.

The participants' accounts also illustrated the ways in which 'visibility' in presentation-based assignments left South-Asian students of the Islamic faith and Black heritage students vulnerable to what they perceived to be anti-Muslim and anti-Black discrimination within the assessment process. To circumvent this, the latter group of students frequently resorted to the strategy of adopting a White performance during presentations, in an attempt to mask their own Blackness to succeed in assessment – what King (2004) connotes as 'playing the White man' (in sporting spaces).

The students' accounts here underscore Ahmed and Cushing's (2021) observation that assessments in HE are constructed around educational gatekeepers' narrow expectation of the cultural currencies, knowledge, resources and networks that students should ideally posses. They conclude that this situation leaves young people who culturally fall outside of this narrow framework, with few options but to modify their language towards specific racialised and classed standards of normality that are set by '[W]hite speakers and listeners' – a process which they define as 'a part of the colonial legacies of linguistic categorisation'. For the most part, however, these resources are likely to be possessed by students who are White and middle class. Above all else then, the accounts shared and discussed here, and in the last 3 chapters, have shown us how this situation means that students who fall outside of this intersected race and classed frame, have to work much harder than their White and middle-class peers to achieve equitable outcomes.

Chapters 2, 3 and 4 centred the students voice and provided thick descriptions of assessment as experienced along the axis of race. In this chapter, I have attempted to provide some discussion on how we might make sense of this theoretically. However, this leaves us with a rather important and yet unanswered question that the second half of this book seeks to address: What can educators do *right now* to mitigate these issues in their practice?

ACKNOWLEDGEMENTS

The author would like to thank Taylor and Francis for allowing the use of material from the following article in this chapter: Campbell, P. I. (2022). Pray(ing) the person marking your work isn't racist: Racialised inequities in HE assessment practice. *Teaching in Higher Education*. https://doi.org/10.1080/14660970.2022.2109805.

PART 2

WHAT DIFFERENCE DOES RACIALLY INCLUSIVE ASSESSMENT MAKE, AND FOR WHO?

6

THE EFFECTS OF RACIALLY INCLUSIVE ASSESSMENT ON THE RACE AWARD GAP AND ON STUDENTS' LIVED EXPERIENCES OF ASSESSMENT

The stories examined in the first half of this book sketched out how students of colour experience exclusion in assessment in three ways: In relation to barriers in pre-assessment support and post-assessment support and barriers that were more directly related to their racialised identities. I used these three emergent themes to form a tri-based framework in which to generate 20 recommendations for Racially Inclusive Assessment Guidance. These were then developed into the *Racially Inclusive Practice in Assessment Guidance Intervention* (henceforth RIPIAG) – see Table 1.

This chapter sketches out the efficacy of the RIPIAG, which was implemented in three HEPs – *The University of Borne, Meadow University* and *Wiseman University*. However, this was not a straightforward process. Firstly, we chose to only test the recommendations for racially inclusive pre-assessment support. This was because many of the recommendations which addressed the more obvious racial barriers in assessment were also connected to issues of transparency, which were addressed in the pre-assessment support guidance. Secondly, feedback processes in most HEPs are tied to

Table 1. Developmental Process From Racially Inclusive Practice in Assessment Guidance to Racially Inclusive Practice in Assessment Guidance Intervention and Resources.

Racially Inclusive Assessment Guidance: Pre-Assessment Support Recommendations	Racially Inclusive Practice in Assessment Guidance	Racially Inclusive Practice in Assessment Guidance Intervention (RIPIAG)
1: Introduce signposts in module guides and weekly schedules for when students might begin to prepare for assessments, especially for students at Level 1 and 2. Or consider introducing formative exercises and activities that prompt students to prepare for assessments	1: Introduce signposts in module guides and weekly schedules for when students might begin to prepare for assessments, especially for students at Level 1 and 2. Or consider introducing formative exercises and activities that prompt students to prepare for assessments	*The Critical Assessment Schedule* *This resource relates to Racially Inclusive Practice in Assessment Guidance Recommendation 1.
2: Introduce more modelling exercises that critically assess examples of previous work	2: Introduce exercises which translate marking criteria jargon into accessible language and provide examples for illustration	*The Critical Assignment Brief* *This resource relates to Racially Inclusive Practice in Assessment Guidance Recommendations 5 and 6.
3: Introduce exercises which translate marking criteria jargon into accessible language and provide examples for illustration	3: Introduce more modelling exercises that critically assess examples of previous work	
4: Introduce more modelling and grading exercises that clearly explain how the marking process works	4: Introduce more modelling and grading exercises that clearly explain how the marking process works	*The Modified Seminar Workshop* *This resource relates to Racially Inclusive Practice in Assessment Guidance Recommendations 2, 3 and 4.
5: The inclusion of an Assignment Brief, or exercises that 'unpack' essay questions (if the assignment question requires unpacking, perhaps rephrase it to avoid unnecessary confusion)	5: The inclusion of an Assignment Brief, or exercises that 'unpack' essay questions (if the assignment question requires unpacking, perhaps rephrase it to avoid unnecessary confusion)	
6: Include FAQs, which might include a 'to do' list and a list of common mistakes	6: Include FAQs, which might include a 'to do' list and a list of common mistakes	*The Active Group Marking Exercise* *This resource relates to Racially Inclusive Practice in Assessment Guidance Recommendations 2, 3 and 4.
7: Introduce more even levels of pre-assessment support for all assessments and across all modules		
8: Pre-assessment support should be employed especially during the transition from FE to HE stages. However, it is worth considering employing these support mechanisms during all, and any, transition stages, where expectations of what is required to secure higher level grade outcomes change, even if the mode of assessment does not.		

extremely rigid and prescriptive quality assurance processes that can only be modified through lengthy administrative processes. Put simply, feedback is operated and managed by quality processes that are unique to each institution, which usually exist beyond the control of individual module convenors. This meant that we could not guarantee consistency in the application of the post-assessment recommendations and thus could not measure their efficacy for making feedback practice more racially inclusive.

The RIPIAG consists of four practical pedagogical resources: The Critical Assignment Schedule (CAS), The Critical Assignment Brief (CAB), The Modified Active Seminar Workshop (MASW) and The Active Group Marking Exercise (AGME) (see Table 1).

The CAS is a detailed timetable that sets out the key points in the assessment process for each assignment, from the start to submission. It also shows precisely when in the semester students should ideally have started and/or completed the various tasks that comprise the assessment.

The CAB is a 3-page document (maximum) that contains at least all of the following information:

- Submission Deadline
- Grade Weighting of Assignment
- Assignment Instructions
- Assignment Questions
- Tips and Essential Things to Include (when completing each assignment question)
- Learning Outcomes
- Referencing Instructions
- What is Academic Misconduct?
- Non/Late Submissions

The MASW consists of a series of (inter)active and group-based learning exercises that cover, at least, the following areas:

- What do I need to get started?
- Structuring the Assignment
- Formulating an Introduction
- Assignment Do's and Don'ts
- Key Advice: What are the differences between stronger and weaker assignments?
- Learning the difference between anecdotal, evidence and critical arguments?

The AGME is a group-based activity where students mark previous scripts. Using a combination of the assessment content covered in the MASW and the marking criteria, students have to come to a consensus about the grade score for each script. In each case, they provide a rationale for the awarded grade using the descriptors in the marking criteria and the lessons learnt in the seminar to justify the grade given. They also must suggest one thing that could be added to improve the assignment, with an example.

The RIPIAG was trialed between September 2021 and December 2022, in six modules, across three partner HEPs, which all had student populations that were made of at least 37% who self-identified as belonging to a minority ethnic background. Only one core module per course could be selected (this was at the discretion of the partner HEP). The final sample consisted of 175 undergraduate students, of which, over 35% were domicile students of colour.

My previous experiences of developing, embedding and evaluating race inclusion interventions in education have shown that their effectiveness as tools for change are negatively influenced by a general lack of standardisation in their application (see Campbell et al., 2022). To avoid this issue, module convenors were provided with training workshops and with templates for each of the four teaching resources, to ensure a more consistent level of embeddedness of the intervention into their modules.

What then was the RIPIAG's capacity to foster a reduction in the race award gap (RAG) in student outcomes? What was its capacity to improve the qualitative experiences of minority ethnic students in assessment? The remainder of this chapter discusses the results of these two tests.

AN EFFECTIVE TOOL FOR REDUCING THE GENERAL RACE AWARD GAP BETWEEN STUDENTS OF COLOUR AND WHITE PEERS

The quantitative data generated from the assessment scores of the 175 students on treated modules showed that the RIPIAG was remarkably effective at reducing the RAG in the sample (see Table 2).

Specifically, Table 2 shows that the average RAG difference between students of colour and those who identified as White across all treated modules was 6.97%. The narrowest gap recorded was 1.25% and the widest 18.70%. In all cases, the RAG on modified modules was below the overall RAG reported at their respective HEPs. In 83% of modified modules, the reported RAG difference was lower than the 8.8% national average that.

To measure what we might describe as the 'differences within difference', we tested the impact of the modified modules on students' assessment performances against their performance on non-treated modules. We also measured the performance of students on the current treated iteration of the module against the performance of students on previous and non-treated iterations of the same module in previous years.

The results showed a similarly positive pattern of efficacy. For example, 66% of treated modules reported narrower RAGs when compared to the average RAG score recorded for all non-treated modules on that course and at that level. Also, all of the treated modules reported narrower gaps when compared to their aggregate performance for the previous 2 years.

Of course, the findings here do not account for important variations that we must 'factor in' when considering the impact and effectiveness of the intervention for reducing the RAG, such as a cohort with an unusually large cluster of stronger or weaker

Table 2. Race Award Gap in Student Assessment Performance on Modified Modules.

University and Module Code	RAG score for Treated Module	Module RAG Average for Previous 2 years	Course RAG at that Level	University RAG
University of Bourne M1	1.25%	6.97%	1.20%	10.0%
University of Bourne M2	1.80%	4.11%	2.85%	10.0%
University of Bourne M3	7.38%	7.63%	−0.30%	10.0%
Meadow University M1	4.70%	30.25%	23.20%	22.0%
Meadow University M2	18.70%	37.0%	20.10%	32.0%
Wiseman University M1	8.0%	10.95%	12.00%	18.6%
Average score	6.97%	16.15%	9.84%	17.1%

students within a particular minority-ethnic group in any given year. Nor does these data account for variations in the overall number of students of colour within any minority-ethnic group in any particular year. Annual variations in each year's cohort, such as these, make it impossible to have exact like for like comparisons between years. They also influence and skew slightly the veracity of the quantitative findings here and potentially in future. They also remind us that it is unlikely and unrealistic to assume that the intervention will lead to a seamlessly consistent and linear annual reduction in RAGs. Nonetheless, the triangulation and repetition of consistent patterns of RAG reduction reported in the performance data from across all modified modules, from different courses, levels and partner HEPs, provide the basis for confidence in the intervention's ability and potential to positively reduce the aggregate RAG.

While the overall patterns of reduction in RAGs on the sample are encouraging, it is important to also note that where disaggregated data for the performance of students from specific minority-ethnic groups were available, in almost all cases, the RAG for Black-heritage students remained wider than those recorded by all other minority groups. Students who self-defined as 'other', which included British East Asian students, reported the lowest RAG and in some cases outperformed White peers. This group was followed by students who self-described as South Asian and then those who defined as 'mixed' (none of whom outperformed White peers). Interestingly, these patterns of effectiveness and limitation of the intervention corroborated with, and were explained in, the qualitative accounts of the student participants.

THE QUALITATIVE IMPACT OF THE RIPIAG ON THE EVERYDAY LIVED EXPERIENCES OF STUDENTS OF COLOUR IN HE ASSESSMENT

The accounts of all students on treated modules compared to those who were on non-treated modules showed that the RIPIAG was almost universal in its ability to enhance Black, South Asian *and* White students' experiences of the assessment process. Interestingly, each resource appeared to provide a different function for facilitating positive change in students' overall learning experiences when it came to assessment.

THE IMPACT OF THE CRITICAL ASSIGNMENT SCHEDULE ON STUDENTS' LIVED EXPERIENCES OF ASSESSMENT

The CAS resource appeared to help students learn the assessment journey in its entirety. It helped them map when in the semester they should ideally start thinking about their assignment question, when to settle on the question, when to have a first draft complete and so on. This training was effective at helping students guard against their own (frequently inaccurate) commonsense schedules for completing their assignments. For example, students remarked that when they first saw that they 'only' had a 1,500- or 2,000-word essay to complete for their assignment, they rationally thought that it would only take them a few days to complete. Consequently, they believed they would only need to start preparing and working on their assignment a few days before its due date – instead of long before that.

More specifically, the CAS was also especially effective for helping students from all backgrounds develop a better understanding of when to begin the process of working on their assignments. The testimonies indicate how this clarity was particularly novel and transformative for students for whom university and, in turn, assessment at the undergraduate level, were new or alien. These were often FIF students and thus were less likely to have access to the kinds of kin- and social-networks that provide the essential 'insider' knowledge that makes it considerably easier to successfully navigate academic life. Without access to what we might describe as a bank of knowledge that is typically hidden from working-class and FIF students, they are often left to rely on their own 'commonsense' solutions to these problems, which often runs contrary to good assessment practice orthodoxy. The following accounts detail some of the ways in which the CAS was especially effective at teaching students how to mitigate these common but often costly miscalculations.

> Like, when we first start, obviously we don't know what's ... to be expected, essentially. So I think it gives us a good idea of how early we should be thinking about assignments. I'm not gonna lie, I have done some assignments, like, last minute. (Kara, Black Student, University of Bourne)

> So, I think it does help in terms of giving us guidance on where we should be starting ... 'Cause we wouldn't have known how much time to put into them ... without that! ... Obviously in the handbook it tells you how many words you have to do. And it's like... all right, 1,500, that's fine. Like, we can do that in two days, no worries. (Tuni, Black Student, University of Bourne)

THE CRITICAL ASSIGNMENT BRIEF AND CHANGES IN STUDENTS' LIVED EXPERIENCES OF ASSESSMENT

The CAB was remarkably effective at enhancing all students' ability to make sense of their assignment questions and specifically on what it wanted them to address. It did this by enhancing their ability to successfully deconstruct assignment questions, that were often verbose. Students remarked that this changed their overall perceptions of assignment questions from instructions that were often unclear and in turn daunting, into a set of succinct instructions that were more straightforward and manageable.

> [On other modules] you don't really know what they're asking for... [But the CAB] helps 'cos then you have a clear idea. I at least have, like, a path... So it does give us that. It creates a little less panic, if you will. And it does help you build your assignment – [It] gives you a starting place... (Fatima, South Asian Student, Meadow University)

> So, I think it's helpful that it gives you the 'write down' of how the essay needs to be laid out ... For me, it helps reduce the stress. Because you can break it down into smaller sections ... Rather than thinking, I've got a 2,500-word essay that I need to do. So, okay, well I can concentrate on this section and then break it down that way. So I think that helps reduce stress as well. (Francis, White Student, Wiseman University)

> I think those [CABs] were quite good because it gave me a sense of what you need to actually talk about. Um, so that was helpful when planning what you were going to say and linking it to the questions that were there. I think it was really good because it just gives

you, like, a bit of a prompt. So, you're not, like, completely clueless about what, where to start. (Mandeep, South Asian Student, University of Bourne)

I looked at [the CAB] and I was like, am I hitting this point? Am I getting that one? Like, it made it a lot easier. Whereas, for example, I'm working on an essay [on another module] now, which is due in a few days. [All we have been given is] just a question [and no CAB]. And ... I'm planning it ... And I'm making points. And I'm [asking myself]: 'is this [what she's writing] really relevant?' (Amy, White Student, Bourne University)

[Without the CAB] It's harder... Yeah, it's like we, kind of, play a guessing game with everything else. Like, with the [assignment for another module] ... I had no idea what I was doing for that one ... (Viv', Black Student, Bourne University)

The stories from students from all three raced groups and all three universities above triangulate to illustrate how remarkably effective the CAB was for providing students with a blueprint for how to deconstruct their assignment questions and for making the minimum knowledge/content requirements that were expected to be to be covered in the assignment task visible to them. This function of the CAB also had a particularly positive impact for raising students' confidence in their ability to succeed and, importantly, on reducing their general feelings of anxiety and stress that were usually brought on by assessment (Boustani, 2023).

The stories of assessment detailed in Chapters 2, 3, 4 and 5 illustrated how students of colour particularly found the language used in assignment questions to be verbose and confusing (and this was connected to wider social factors and not the result of any inherent inability). This made knowing what specific knowledge or skills the task wanted them to demonstrate difficult. To some, this made assignments and essay questions high jeopardy. The participants who took part in the evaluation echoed similar barriers to comprehension and resultant anxieties.

The inclusion of the exposition within the CAB helped them to deconstruct the instruction and, in turn, significantly reduced the jeopardy that typically accompanied the assignment questions reported by students of colour. Additionally, students remarked that having a resource which clearly outlined what each question was specifically asking was effective in reducing the time they spent on trying to 'figure out' what the question wanted them to demonstrate. In doing so, it enabled students to maximise the time and energy spent on showcasing the required knowledge or skill. This also meant that they were less likely to be faced with the prospect of having to choose between answering a question that they understood over a question on a topic that they were particularly interested in, passionate about, or knowledgeable on.

> [W]ith a broader question, you, kind of, need an, an assignment brief to guide you 'cos anyone can go on a different tangent. And then you don't know which one's right and which one's wrong! (Jenni, Black Student, University of Bourne)

> Yeah, I found [the CAB] helpful. Like, even before I started [my assignment], it gave me an idea of what each question entailed. So, I could choose a question... and have more idea what question to do. [Rather] than if I had just been [given] the question [without any exposition] ... It's not like the plan's done for you ... You're able to pick out the one [question] you want ... 'Cause, if it wasn't broken-down like that ... I don't think I'd be that confident in doing it. (Alicia, South Asian Student, Meadow University)

> [The CAB had] tips on how to approach a question. That helped a lot 'cause it's like ... okay: 'This is what the question's asking you to do.' And I think that helped 'cause the whole guidance thing was more like,

> okay: 'So this is roughly how you should approach the question.' And, you know, this is where you should be going with it. So, yeah, that helped a lot! (Dee, Black Student, University of Bourne)

Importantly, the CAB was effective for reducing students' dependency on lecturing staff to complete their work. Consequently, this meant that they relied less on direct input from staff for reassurance about whether-or-not they were 'on the right track' for success, and it enhanced their ability to function as independent learners (which was corroborated by the staff testimonies examined in Chapter 7). This also meant that students (and especially those from raced backgrounds) no longer had to reach out to lecturers who they were often not comfortable in seeking out. Nor did they have to endure the psychological drama of having to overcome any sense of vulnerability that came with exposing any perceived lack of understanding for the task and any negative judgements that might be made about them.

> Yes, so you've still got something to refer to back to. You've got the structure in front of you. Even if I don't go back to the lecturer, I could look at that. (Mo', South Asian Student, Wiseman University)

> [The CAB] kind of shows you what someone expects from that assignment. But for the other modules that we had to do an essay with, I think it was just harder because it was just the questions. And even the questions were just very hard to understand what they meant. And there wasn't really any other advice that it gave us after that. (Mandeep, South Asian Student, University of Bourne)

> I feel like the assignment brief was very useful. The fact that the question was there, but then it also broke down the question for you, made it easier for you to do your introduction. Because you knew what you had to talk about, and then style your essay ... And then, at the bottom [of the CAB], it would have an extra point,

> *which is the stronger essays would do 'blah blah blah'. I thought that part, as well, was very useful because it, kind of, allows you to try and push yourself to see if you can reach what those stronger essays would do. (Jason, Black Student, University of Bourne)*

Concerns centred on the negative effects of too much support are often raised by educators, who proffer that assignment support reduces students' ability to be innovative or to demonstrate creativity and individual excellence in their assessed work. The following student accounts, however, point to an opposite outcome brought about by the intervention.

> *I think with the creativ[ity] thing it's like [the CAB] does both. Because it's like if you have less guidance, its obviously [leaves you] open to more avenues [to explore] ... At the same time, you're also stressing about, is this the correct avenue I should be going down? (Valerie, Black Student, University of Bourne)*

> *[H]aving some sort of guide when you're writing an essay is so important! It just helps you. It just helps you guide your thinking. It's not supposed to stop you from adding anything else. Like, as long as it connects and is valid ... Then it's fine. (Simone, Black Student, Wiseman University)*

> *Not to name names or point fingers, but in a certain other module we had to write an essay. It was incredibly vague [question] on what the essay should even be about. That was traumatising to say the least! Because ... If it's not specific, in order to guide your thinking, then you could end up writing an essay that maybe is not even related and then perhaps you get a bad grade, because [the answer] was not supposed to be on that point. (Lexi, White Student, University of Bourne)*

> *I think [the CAB] definitely helped guide my thinking. Seeing especially where it said to address the*

> limitations. I already thought to do that, but seeing it written down, like, confirmed it for me and helped me to stay on that track and confirm what I was going to do. And it just helped me have more confidence when I was writing because I knew that it was on the focus of what [the lecturer] expected from us and wanted. (Jo, White Student, University of Bourne)

Including the 'wrong thing' or going 'off topic' was one of the most commonly rehearsed reasons for the participants' reluctance to be expressive in their assignments in other modules. Consequently, the CAB enhanced students' confidence to be even more creative within the confines of the assignment, instead of stifling it. The CAB, in addition to the other RIPIAG exercises and resources discussed throughout, were successful in making the parameters of the assignment more transparent for all students. In doing so, the CAB helped to make clear the pedagogical conditions and boundaries of the task. One effect of this was that it enabled students to feel more confident and reassured of what to, and what not to include when approaching their assignments. Put simply, the CAB provided the platform for students to be even more creative because it removed the fear of going off task – and ultimately failing their assignments.

THE EFFECT OF THE MODIFIED ACTIVE SEMINAR WORKSHOPS ON STUDENTS' EVERYDAY EXPERIENCES OF ASSESSMENT

Overall, the testimonies illustrated the effectiveness of the MASW for facilitating a deeper and more accurate understanding of the assessment process for students of colour and for all students more widely. This was achieved through a combination of social and dialogic learning.

The MASW consisted of a series of 'active learning' activities 'which provide module specific and 'hands on' assessment support, which made clear what it is that makes work successful and how this relates to the marking criteria' (Campbell, 2022b, p. 8). The accounts below demonstrate how the active learning activities within the modified seminars directly transformed students' experiences of assessment from something which was 'individual' to one which was much more social and dialogic.

> *Not everybody understands marking criteria exactly the same... I think engaging in group work helped a lot to reflect off each other. (Deli, Black Student Wiseman University)*

> *It helped to see multiple perspectives – but also [to see] multiple ways of doing the assignment. (Delorus, Black Student, University of Bourne)*

> *You, like, have your own ideas, but then when you can speak with others [students], it just develops them [their ideas and comprehension] more. And with certain modules, you don't really feel like you can do that. (Stacy, White Student, University of Bourne)*

> *I feel that when you're just doing your assignment, you're just in a bubble [on their own] and you don't realise it. (Niki, South Asian Student, University of Bourne)*

The testimonies highlight that the active learning exercises required students to explain (the aspect of the) assessment to each other, challenge each other's response and then required them to either modify or defend their views to reach a group consensus. This approach to learning aligns with what Alexander (1996) described as 'dialogic' pedagogy. This is the idea that effective learning is achieved through a process of 'meaningful talk' (Alexander, 1996), similar to that described above. A 'deeper' knowledge/understanding is reached through justification, challenge/defence, modification and then re-comprehension. Importantly, meaningful dialog can only take place if both learners are of relative equal status (if any two people can be equal). Put another way, meaningful talk cannot take place between lecturer and student because the power imbalance removes the student's ability to engage in 'meaningful talk'. This is because they will typically accept the lecturer's assertion as valid. This is what usually happens, for example, when assessment learning takes place through a more transmissive and passive mode of delivery, such as in a lecture. However, when the dialog takes place between peers in a group exercise, students are more inclined to engage in meaningful dialog where, using evidence, they discuss, challenge, justify, modify or confirm their understanding.

This approach is routinely employed in compulsory education and in HEPs to varying degrees, especially in relation to the kinds of comprehension building exercises employed within seminars. In contrast to their general taught educative experiences in HE, assessments were things which students largely did on their own and in silos (unless it was a group assignment).

It is unsurprising given this background that the students here found the siloed nature of learning, and of doing assessments, to be alien, stressful and often unhelpful. Conversely, they reported considerably higher levels of comfort, comprehension and confidence when learning assignment literacy through the more social and dialogic approach taken within the modified seminars.

The MASW also enhanced students' ability to make sense of marking criteria and learning objectives and turn them into meaningful instructions. For example, the Black, South Asian and White students surveyed in Chapter 2, 3, and 4 and here, all reported that they often found the terminology used in their module's Learning Objectives and in the marking criteria to be opaque, abstract and in some cases incomprehensible.

They all recognised that terms such as 'critical argument', 'logical structure' and 'anecdotal evidence' were all important – and frequently rehearsed – 'things' that needed to be demonstrated or avoided. However, in practice these terms meant very little to them when completing their own portfolios, coursework or exams. The testimonies below demonstrate some of the ways in which the exercises within the modified seminars were transformative in helping students to translate and, in turn, 'see' and learn what this terminology meant and looked like when it came to completing their own assessments.

There was one bit where [the seminar] actually - as silly as it sounds - explained what critical analysis was. So I've had formatives before where they've [other lecturers have] been like you need to be more critical. But she actually gave an example [and exercises to learn it]. And as silly as that sounds, [now] that [I have seen what critical analysis is, it] makes so much more sense. (Simone, Black Student, Wiseman University)

Not everybody can interpret that document [marking criteria] in the same way... Therefore [the seminar] gives us different options and different ways to understand what we need to do to receive a First. (Nisha, Black Student, Meadow University)

There's so [much] jargon in the mark schemes ... and with[in the] Learning Objectives... [Other Lecturers will] say follow the Learning Objectives... And sometimes I look at them, [and] I'm like, I still don't know exactly what that means! So, yeah, kind of going through it [in the seminar helps] ... (Becki, White Student, Meadow University)

So, now we know [how to] write and meet the Learning Objectives that are given to get the high[er] grades. Whereas, if we didn't have that, and we just got given the assignment to do, I don't think, ... because I've got dyslexia personally, so I don't think I would have understood how to structure each paragraph and get the higher marks [without the seminar activities]. I probably would have 40 or 50% max, if I didn't get this! [the help in the seminar]. (Jack, White Student, Wiseman University)

The seminars also enhanced students' ability to breakdown the assignment from a large and daunting undertaking, into a set of smaller and more manageable sub-activities. Students from all three different racial backgrounds and across all partner HEPs reported that they often found the prospect of completing assignments (on other modules) to be 'overwhelming'.

Students asserted that the new seminars were especially helpful for modifying their attitudes towards assessment. The active learning exercises within the MASW were particularly effective at enhancing students' ability to identify, separate out – or 'breakdown' – the 'total' sum of the assignment task (essay, presentation, report and so on) into a series of smaller and in turn, less daunting set of actions (e.g. 'Structuring the Assignment', 'Formulating an Introduction', 'Learning the difference between anecdotal arguments, evidenced arguments and critical arguments', and so on). Furthermore, it provided active and group-based exercises for each section, which taught students how to complete each self-contained component of the assignment. It also (actively) taught them what constituted a stronger or weaker sub-section and why it was.

This deconstructed and more scaffolded approach to completing assignments acted as a 'baseline' 'checklist'. It was, for some, an essential 'kit' for 'surviving' the assessment process. In almost all cases, it was seen as a core contributor for success, and for making them feel at ease and confident when doing their assessments in modified modules.

> *The [seminar] broke-it-down essentially. Like, okay, this is what you need to tackle. These are the questions that you needed to ask yourself. That's helped. I think that's one of the reasons why we have the grades we have ... [W]e've done okay [in our assessment] because of those templates and that guidance. I think it's helped a lot. (Trevone, Black Student, University of Bourne)*

> *[The seminar] really breaking-it-down. I liked the group work as well. It was really helpful. (Sumaya, South Asian Bangladeshi-heritage Student, University of Bourne)*

> *The workshops and seminars that we've had around assessments have been really helpful. [B]ecause it gave us like a baseline on what to do. Seeing, like, a structure ... it really helped for me to form my own essay. Like the [others have already] said, about [being] thrown in at the*

deep end [on other modules]. It didn't feel like that [with the seminar]. It felt like we had that support and it was very helpful. (Stacy, White Student, University of Bourne)

I think it was good having the seminar on, specifically, the essay we had because it was almost like a checklist when you're going back and referring to it. Making sure I was on the right lines just made me feel more confident about my actual essay when I was writing, where another module didn't have that support. And I was, kind of... second-guessing what I was writing. I wasn't too sure if was on the right track! (Sam, White Student, University of Bourne)

I liked the: 'how to structure your essays' [part of the workshop]. Like breaking-it-down on what is a good paragraph, [and] what is not. I liked that. (Delorus, Black Student, University of Bourne)

'Cause I'm more of a visual learner, I've got more of a picture in my head of how to lay it out [and] what to include... What to put in the main body. How to link everything back... Like, through the example paragraphs. This is an example of an anecdotal [argument]... (Belle, White Student, Meadow University)

THE IMPACT OF THE ACTIVE GROUP MARKING EXERCISE ON STUDENTS' EXPERIENCES OF ASSESSMENT

Testimonies indicated that the AGME had high efficacy for developing Black, South Asian and White students' comprehensions of assessment from being able to complete the smaller compartmentalised aspects of the assignments (learnt in the modified seminar workshops – see above) to comprehending how these self-contained and dislocated aspects all joined together to form a coherent narrative in a full assignment.

> *[The exercise] puts it in perspective. Like oh! That's a 70 or that's a 60. And then you could think: 'Oh there's the references and that's something that I can use in my own words'. And then put it in to get that higher mark ... So yeah, I think it puts [the whole assignment] in[to] more perspective [and makes what it looks like] more clearer. What they're looking for. (Hena, South Asian Student of the Islamic Faith, Wiseman University)*

> *Sometimes when a tutor's explaining something or a lecturer's explaining something, it can get a bit muddled. I'm a visual learner, so listening is really hard for me ... But when I see it ... It's like that makes way more sense to me... I can apply what you said. (Natalie, White Student, Meadow University)*

The exercises also appeared to enhance students' ability to better understand the module specific expectations of the assignment and mitigate against things like inter-marker variables. These are the potential and different ways of 'doing' the sum or aspects of the assignment that can often vary and are dependent on the preferences of individual lecturers (such as the differences in what is expected in an 'introduction' or a 'conclusion' that may differ between markers). This issue was cause for high anxiety across all student groups.

> *Being able to look at an example answer, especially with your first assignment. Or even going forward, because it sets the basis of where you should be at, when you're going further. You're able to add more information to that because you [see] what's expected of you. (Sam, White Student, University of Bourne)*

> *I do find example essays and how it's done well. I find those good, because I find, like, different lecturers expect different things. (Belle, White Student, Meadow University)*

Students remarked that the AGME was also particularly useful for helping them to see, learn and know what assignments at different levels looked like. Additionally, it was also helpful for improving their ability to see and discuss the different ways in which they might approach the task, and the different ways in which assignments were structured.

For students who were unsure of how to approach the task, they proffered that the exercise helped them to organise their thoughts. It also helped them to structure their ideas and formulate how they might approach the assignment activity. The comments below illustrate some of the ways in which the exercises appeared to be particularly useful to students when they were confronted with modes of assessment which were completely new, or for when the expectations of what constituted a higher-grade response had changed from one year to the next.

> *I think for me, it definitely helped to structure [my work] and I found [it helped me to see] how it should be laid out. (Dal', South Asian Student, Wiseman University)*

> *One thing I always struggled with personally is actually writing my ideas on a piece of paper. Like, the style of writing. And when I did it [the marking exercise], I thought okay, this is the difference! This is how they portray their ideas. This is how you're meant to structure it. (Asifa, South Asian Student of the Islamic Faith, Meadow University)*

> *It's just [seeing] the ideas that you [can] implement into your work ... does help you. Even for me to start my essay 'cause I never know how to start my essay... Like, I never even know how to end my essay. It's always the introduction, the conclusion for me [that's the hardest]. The middle bit I'm fine with. (Sasha, South Asian Student of the Islamic Faith, Meadow University)*

The AGME also had a direct impact on improving students' perceptions of their own efficacy to complete their assignment and importantly on their confidence of being able to produce higher level responses.

The overwhelming majority of participants remarked that the marking to the grading criteria component of the marking exercise challenged their instinctive ideas of what constituted good assessment practice and excellence at the undergraduate level. This was often at odds with best assessment practice as set out within the marking criteria and learnt in the seminar activity.

Some students admitted to having to fight against their original ideas of what assessment excellence looked like when marking previous assignments for the first time (and even after taking part in the active seminar). Their instinct here was to score exemplar work much lower and more harshly than the module convenor. In turn, the grading exercises helped underscore the lessons learnt in the MASW. It also facilitated a more accurate comprehension of what was required for assignments to score in each grade boundary.

Subsequently, the exercise provided a triple function. It reinforced a more accurate comprehension of what constitutes higher level work (learnt in the seminar). It helped students to see that what constituted higher standard work was often lower than their initial expectations, which served to reassure them of their own aptitude and ability to succeed. Importantly, it reassured them that producing a higher-level response was not beyond them.

In turn, the activity had a direct impact on raising student confidence. This appeared to particularly be an issue for students of colour or who were White and self-Identified as working-class. These are students who have historically found HE an alien space, which runs contrary to their own race and classed habitus (See Campbell, 2022b).

> *It was very easy to know where we'd be scoring ... [against] those assignments. (Del', Black Student, Meadow University)*

> *I would say that when we had those essays, it made me feel a lot better about the assignment. Because the ones that I thought were bad were actually quite good. And it made me feel a bit better thinking that, you know, if I was to do an essay to this standard, I wouldn't fail. And I just think it was like a, a big, like, reliever when I read*

> *them. I think it was very helpful to, like, understand where I could put myself in terms of those essays (scores). (Millie, White Student, Meadow University)*
>
> *I just think it helps because I was a bit stressed at first, but seeing someone else's work and realising it is actually manageable and it can be done, that helped. (Cassie, White Student, Wiseman University)*

Lastly, the exercises were particularly effective at improving students' ability to guard against another widely held inaccurate 'commonsense' assumption of what good assessment practice was. Many students of colour remarked that they were still the first in their family to go to university and that when in the Whitened university space, they tended to seek out and socialise with people from similar raced and class backgrounds. Rehearsing the comments made by the Black and South Asian student participants in Chapters 3 and 4, participants from racialised backgrounds here also commented that they would only seek out their lecturers for assignment support as a very 'last resort'. Indeed, no students who were Black reported being comfortable going to staff for assessment assistance at all. As such, students here reported that typically they instead often drew on kin and friendship networks for answers to issues relating to their assessments – the course WhatsApp group was often a key resource here. In many cases, these networks often consisted of people from similar social or raced backgrounds to them and who were equally as unfamiliar with how HE and assessment worked (see Campbell, 2020). This meant that, in most cases, solutions to assignment problems offered would often be anecdotal or commonsense.

One popular position originally proffered by students, for example, was that cramming in as much information as possible, learnt during the module, into a single assessment response – what they described as a 'scatter gun' or 'waffly' approach – was a formula for success. Ironically, of course, the reverse is often the case: that to score highly, students often have to demonstrate depth and not breadth of understanding. However, it is not difficult to see why 'intuitively', this approach might be thought to be one which demonstrates high(er) levels of engagement, knowledge and comprehension.

> [The Lecturer] showed us one [essay] that was really extensive... And then one that was really short. But the shorter one got more marks! Because it still went into detail, but the [previous] one didn't go into detail... So, you can kind of tell... Not 'cause of how big it is, but because it needs to back up your point - Your explanation. So all of that, I feel like it just really helped. (Sasha, South Asian Student of the Islamic Faith, Meadow University)

> I think, looking at the different assignments and looking at the different grades that each one got, you compare it to what your writing is like. So, if you read through it and it turns out to be 40%, you know that from the other higher examples, what you sort of need to [do to improve] ... your writing, to achieve that high grade. (Francis, White Student, Wiseman University)

> I would say that particular exercise when we had to mark the different essays didn't necessarily tell me what I should do to get a first, but it told me what I shouldn't do to not get a first, if that was the right way to say it? ... It didn't show me what I needed to do, it showed me what I didn't need to do. (Stevie, Black Student, Meadow University)

> Before, I used to waffle in my introductions. And I just found out that's not what you need to do! (Sonya, South Asian Student of the Islamic Faith, Meadow University)

Perhaps above all else, these final examples illustrate how the AGME directly enhanced students' ability to mitigate against these kinds of miscalculations. It also provided a direct reference point for students to recognise the strengths and weaknesses in their own assignments and assessment practice.

SOME CONCLUDING COMMENTS: THE CONTRASTING EXPERIENCES OF ASSESSMENT BETWEEN RACIALISED STUDENTS ON MODIFIED MODULES AND STUDENTS OF COLOUR ON NON-MODIFIED MODULES

The testimonies throughout clearly demonstrate the cross-racial impact of the intervention for improving the assessment experiences of students from all three racial backgrounds examined. Importantly, they provide an empirical account for how each resource contributed to a more transparent experience, which benefitted and enhanced all students' understandings of when to start, what to do, how to do it and what assessment success looks like. However, I want to finish by showing how the intervention also made a noteworthy and specific difference in the assessment experience of domicile undergraduate students from global majority backgrounds, when contrasted with students of colour who were not on treated modules.

Students of colour who were on modified modules were noticeably keen to press that the intervention had made them more clear-eyed and confident about what assignments at different levels required and looked like.

> *I think we both kind of knew the ballpark of where we were gonna get all of our grades [when I submitted] ... I think it was very much like, like I knew where my weaknesses were immediately, kind of thing. So I was like, okay, have I developed the point fully? Like, I think I could tell where I'd done well and I could tell where I hadn't done as well... And it's like, have I answered this the best way? Maybe I haven't referenced enough or I haven't developed this point fully, etc. So I think it was made very clear. I think that's the reason why the grades weren't a surprise ... (Dionne, Black Student, University of Bourne)*

> *I think that when the paper laid out what the grading system was [taught to us], it helped us a lot, too. 'Cause,*

> we didn't even know how our assessments were going to be graded until we came to that seminar. (Ranjeet, South Asian Student, University of Bourne)

> So, yeah, I like everything on there [the RIPIAG] to be fair. So it does help us in that sense. So, we don't need to go to him [the lecturer] 'cos he's already provided it. (Asifa, South Asian Student of the Islamic Faith, Meadow University)

> When you get a grade that isn't what you think relates to your effort… [We now know] that it's not because the lecturer doesn't [like you]… You can actually start to see how and why you got that grade … (Dee, Black Student, University of Bourn)

The accounts of the students of colour in our sample clearly illustrate how the increase in transparency of the assessment process brought about by the RIPIAG was transformative. It that Black and South Asian students better understood how they were being assessed and what was required to achieve desired grades. It also facilitated a stronger sense of trust between faculty and students of colour.

This was in stark contrast to the experience of Black and South Asian students on non-treated modules who, as we discussed in Chapters 3, 4 and 5, were often unaware of exactly how they were assessed. This situation led to these students of colour having to speculate when assessment outcomes did not match their effort, which often fostered feelings of racial foul play and distrust (see Campbell, 2022).

Lastly, the testimonies below remind us of the multiplicity of wider and acute anti-Black challenges and barriers in HE that impact negatively on Black students' chances of achieving outcome parity in assessment.

> When it comes to academic writing, like I need a lot of reassurance, like I think it might be just me being anxious … Yeah, it [the RIPIAG] helps. But it's not

> the only [thing I need] ... I need more! If that makes sense? (Nisha, Black Student, Meadow University)

> [The module convenor of the modified module] is the only one, or one of the only lecturers, that actually supports you. In terms of tries to explain things in different ways because he understands, or I can only assume that he understands, that not everybody understands academic language the same way ... And he's one of the only people that will do it! So if you wanna say dumb it down, yeah, he does dumb down the mark scheme for us... Whereas I've had [other] lecturers that you can tell from their background, that they don't have that ability to, I'm not gonna say dumb down again, but ... to make things transparent. Because that academic language is their normal language... (Del', Black Student, Meadow University)

Importantly, these accounts also showcase some of the limitations of the intervention's ability to mitigate against the anti-Black inequities that exist outside of modules that contribute to the stymieing of Black students from achieving grade outcome parity with other raced students and White peers, such as a lack of Black role modules in faculties and in leadership. Or in student well-being services that have historically struggled to 'reach' Black students when they experience mental ill-health (Boustani, 2023). Black participants asserted that if the academe was serious about trying to eliminate RAGs, then it needed to also address these wider anti-Black barriers too.

> I think if those ... [RIPIAG] resources and the help we get in this module was [course]-wide, it'd be really useful. But I think again, [the ability to do well in assessments is also] based on your attendance or based on... how [well] you know your [and get on with your] lecturer, as well! (Del', Black Student, Meadow University)

> I think yeah [the RIPIAG] increase[d] my confidence a bit ... I think it's good. It most definitely will help if it

was all across [all our modules]. But I don't think that's the only thing that needs to be included! (Kerri, Black Student, Wiseman University)

[The intervention is helpful] 'cause, in a sense, you don't have to worry about not understanding what you need to do [in the assessment] if that makes sense ... It takes away one struggle! 'Cause now you just have to worry about understanding your course and translating that into a first... So, yeah, it just takes away that issue [but not all of them]. (Nisha, Black Student, Meadow University)

7

RACIALLY INCLUSIVE ASSESSMENT AND ACADEMIC TEACHING STAFF

In what ways had working with the Racially Inclusive Practice in Assessment Guidance Intervention improved academic staffs' understandings of the ways in which their assessment practice is experienced unevenly by students of colour? How had the intervention enhanced teaching practice, and what changes had staff seen in their students' attitudes to, feelings about and performances in assessment? These questions shape the following discussion in this final findings chapter.

THE EFFECTIVENESS OF THE RIPIAG AS A TOOL FOR IMPROVING EDUCATORS' UNDERSTANDING OF RACIAL INEQUITIES IN ASSESSMENT

The testimonies highlighted that prior to completing the race inclusion in assessment training, teaching participants' original ideas of what constituted decolonising work were often narrow. To 'decolonise' was largely considered to be something that applied to modifying curriculum content and, in turn, redressing the ways in which HE curricula in the UK typically prioritised certain voices, canons and viewpoints (and the related racialised power imbalances). Put simply, for staff, decolonising work was primarily an exercise in pluralising course content.

> *I think decolonizing is bound to knowledge and power. So, we are thinking about, or at least being very aware and critical of, who has power in certain situations to define a topic. [Or] to define what is the canon [and] the way of doing research.* (Lecturer, State University)

> *It is a place which only presents certain knowledges, certain histories and prioritises those. It presents those [stories] as the authority over others.* (Lecturer, University of Bourne)

> *[Before taking part in this, decolonizing] meant two strands for me, I guess. One, was about trying to diversify the curriculum in terms of bringing in voices from people of colour. Bringing in resources written by people of colour ... The other strand is about acknowledging and illuminating the ways in which ... colonialism ... or White privilege ... has been enacted throughout history and the impact that has had on our curriculum.* (Lecturer, Wiseman University)

> *So I might say [decolonizing] involves changing your literature. Looking at who the authors are. Looking at the content. Looking at the history.* (Lecturer, University of Bourne)

Against this, the decision to re-frame the project from one about decolonising to an exercise concerned with making practice racially inclusive had a transformative impact for the participants. From the outset, it facilitated a broader conversation and comprehension of what, how and where the undergraduate education that they delivered might work unequally for students of colour. For example:

[Being] racially inclusive is about the person's race ... [and] listening to those who are racially marginalised. Listening to those who are not included. Making sure they have the space and opportunity. And that it's fed [into our practice] either collaboratively, in a co-production [or] co-design ... [So t]hat they feel included. (Lecturer, University of Bourne)

['Racial Inclusion'] It's made me think about racial inequality in a different way. That it's not just where I'm on the curriculum? It's also about ... those enactments of privilege. (Lecturer, Wiseman University)

Exploring race inequities in education through the frame of 'racial inclusion' instead of decolonising enhanced the ability of the educationalists in our sample to think more broadly and outside of the 'box'. It stimulated a wider range of thinking that enabled them to start to think *beyond* course content as the primary site and cause of race exclusion in taught programmes. It enabled staff to begin to consider how things such as the structures, processes and practices that wrap around their modules can also contain specific race-based barriers too.

Importantly, working with the intervention specifically and directly enhanced participants ability to recognise *racial inequities in assessment*. Some reported that they had previously considered that assessment *might* contain some racially exclusionary processes, but thus far, this had only been in an ephemeral way. Their thinking here was typically in relation to how the language used in assessment might present barriers for some students – although, as yet, none had quite worked out *how* or why this might be a particular issue for students of colour or specifically related to assessment.

I was interested in how students might not do as well from non-white backgrounds, but I hadn't beyond, sort of thinking about, you know, the topics that they could do essays in my modules. I hadn't really thought about the form of assessment or the assessment support before, in terms of racialised and ethnic identities ... For me, [working with the RIPIAG] has really helped me to sort of

understand ... And it's completely changed my understanding of assessment and the role it plays in terms of inequities and things like that. Yeah, hands down!
(Lecturer, Meadow University)

I hadn't really thought about the ways in which all the processes effect assessment. The assumptions of what students can and can't do. What kind of currencies and capitals they bring ... The kind of support available in assessment. The kind of feedback in assessment. How all of these kinds of things ... make the process of navigating assessment much easier for you know, for White majority students. And this isn't *something that comes out of ... some inherent link to their skin colour. It comes from when we think about the kinds of independent activities that students have to do in preparation for the assessment ... Which students are gonna have the time to do this? Just take, for example, when we talk about ... if you don't come to class, then you're not gonna get all the information on the assessment. Well, OK. What students are gonna be those that are most likely to be travelling? What students are gonna be most likely to be those that have care responsibilities? What students are those that are likely to kind of have all those other social conditions that make attendance difficult? ... So, you know all of these processes effect students of colour in assessment. But you know, prior to this [process], I hadn't really joined the dots.*
(Lecturer, University of Bourne)

The lecturers' experiences of attending the training workshops, working through the guidance and embedding the RIPIAG intervention into their practice had a more profound and longer-term impact than just altering their modules. It had also helped make them more familiar with, and able to identify, some of the complex and multiple ways in which assessment success and grade outcomes were also, and often, predicated on various currencies that certain raced groups were more or less likely to possess. It also improved their understanding of how racial exclusion worked in their own assessment practice.

Importantly, some White participants were keen to press how the RIPIAG guidance and training workshops enabled them to engage in a process of critical self-reflection of their own complicity as part of an academe that excludes students of colour, in a way that was constructive, useful and did not make them feel guilty.

> *It's given me a better understanding, without me feeling attacked as a White person. To recognise that my practice and also the practice of the institutions that I've worked at. That I work in. Are in many ways institutionally racist, and do have elements of oppression in there ... I think becoming comfortable with the fact that as a White person I have White privilege, and I've always had White privilege, and I will always have White privilege, and recognising how that's enacted within higher education, and how I can challenge that within my practice. I feel like this project has helped me on a journey that I was already on, [and] that I wanted to be on. (Lecturer, Wiseman University)*

AN EFFECTIVE TOOL FOR HELPING STAFF TO MOVE FROM 'INCLUSION' DISCOURSE TO RACIALLY INCLUSIVE ASSESSMENT PRACTICE

Participants explained that universities were placing increasing importance on reducing the RAG. They noted that while their own institutions were developing ever-more sophisticated tools for identifying quantitative gaps in the assessment outcomes between White students and students of colour, they were less forthcoming when it came to providing staff with specific instructions and guidance for how to address these exclusions in taught and assessment practice (beyond repeated calls to decolonise their practice). This meant that when instructed to decolonise their practice by their institutions, staff often had little idea of what this looked like in practice.

This situation often left practitioners feeling 'lost' and 'helpless' with regards to how and where to start to make changes in their modules and related assessment practice. These anxieties were compounded by the annual publication of school- and course-level data that often showed the widening and unequal quantitative-experiences between students of colour and White peers on their programmes and in their modules. Frustrations were also caused by time-based pressures, such as not having enough time to reflect on or to modify their modules *to the extent that would ideally want or in a way that was meaningful.*

Against this situation, staff proffered that working with the RIPIAG helped them to plug this gap in institutional direction and support, and provided them with clear guidance and prompts for change. Described by some as 'a blueprint' for change, the RIPIAG enhanced their ability to see and to respond rapidly and meaningfully to the racial inequities that manifest in their assessment practice. This was described as 'empowering', for some.

> *I think some of these things were in the back of my mind, but I hadn't really put together a plan of how I could support students who were kind of going through it. So this ... gave me an opportunity to actually put some things into practice that I that politically committed to ... And yeah, like empowered me. It gave me very concrete tools that I could put into place.* (Lecturer, University of Bourne)

> *I was given the modules last-minute-dot-com. [The RIPIAG] was accessible and easy for me to quickly implement without having to think: 'God, do I need to go through curriculum changes?' I think that's helpful.* (Lecturer, University of Bourne)

> *What I found really beneficial with the [RIPIAG] project is that the recommendations are really specific in terms of pedagogical practice. They're not vague at all, which sometimes can be the case, I think, with [decolonizing] research. They're very specific ... Personally, as*

> a lecturer, I find them so helpful just in developing my own pedagogical practice and helping me to really reflect on how I, as an educator, can make my students as comfortable as possible with assessment. (Lecturer, Wiseman University)

> I'd say, as a whole, there's very little training in relation to [making our practice racially inclusive]. There's a focus on gaps. But not a clear focus on the different ways in which these gaps can be tackled. And certainly this project's focus on assessment specifically is very much a useful tool in addition to a range of other tools. (Lecturer, Meadow University)

Participants who were non-race specialists asserted that they often found the language and terminology used in race inclusion discourse to be a particular barrier that inhibited some from making change – or knowing what positive change looked like in practice. It was often vague and amorphous. The training here was especially helpful for translating complicated inclusion discourse into actionable instruction.

They argued that this was unlike other inclusion-based initiatives rolled out by HEPs, such as Curriculum Consultants, 'starting a conversation' or Reverse Mentoring. The purpose and measurable difference made by these interventions on changing their practice and making it more inclusive were not always obvious to them, beyond showing White staff the trauma that their students of colour routinely experience in HE. By contrast, the guidance here had a more obvious function and use-value for staff. It helped them to operationalise complex language into visible change in their taught content, exercises and lessons, as illustrated in the following lengthy quotes:

> I think the guidance is really helpful on the number of levels. One: Anything that gives you some clear... considerations for practice is always helpful in the hectic nature of the academic year... This is one of the problems with the conversation on race and inclusion. It's often quite nebulous in terms of what do

things like 'having an inclusive curriculum' [actually] look like? Where do you even start? What does that look like when you're putting together a module for the semester? So it was really helpful in that it provided clear instructions. And Two: The framework ... helped really focus ... your mindset when you're putting this together. What do I need to think about before they [students] even get to the assessment. And then, what do I need to think about after the assessment. And then, what are the kinds of things that I'm doing during this entire process that might impact unevenly on different students ... Even for those, like me, that are quite well versed in the practice of theorizing and conceptualizing race, the guidance for giving us something as a reference point as to what good practice looks like and something to continually go back to and evolve. I think that was really helpful in just providing a schemata for putting this together. (Lecturer, University of Bourne)

I care about students in higher education. So, I've read a lot of journal [articles], and, you know, research and 'blah, blah, blah' ... And the conclusions are always, you know!: 'Well actually, it's higher education that needs to change and not the students that need to change. And we need to fit around them, not they need to fit around us.' Which is lovely in a really vague way. But doesn't necessarily help me as an educator know specifically what to change in my practice to make things better ... Um, and that's a frustration that I have often with journals [articles] and with research. Is that this is wonderful, but what I need is actually the same as what students need. Actual, specific, clear recommendations. Kind of bullet pointed out that these are the things that you can do to help in this area. And that was the key thing for the project for me: It was the clarity of the interventions, and the recommendations. (Lecturer, Wiseman University)

Lastly, staff were keen to press that working with the RIPIAG had shifted their perceptions of assessment from activities that were standalone and that existed outside of the taught curriculum to a skill set or knowledge-base that needed to be cultivated and developed throughout their students' undergraduate journey. Training students in the business of assessment was no longer viewed as something outside of the curriculum. Staff now saw it very much as an important part of the curriculum in all modules that needed to be meaningfully taught to their students. Assessment training was a core part of *their responsibility* as effective educators in the same way that it was their responsibility to teach students course content.

> *So, what we're trying to do is really... move assessment into the learning process... Often, when we teach, we think of course content as the stuff that we need to teach our students, but the assessment is something that exists outside of that, particularly at the module level. We might have a standalone module that deals with assessment... But what we're trying to do and clearly articulate is really to recognise that the learning process is also about learning how to do assessment at undergraduate level. What often has happened in the past is that there's been a gap around that, and that's been left for students to really figure out on their own.* (Lecturer, University of Bourne)

> *[I now know that] assessment isn't this big, scary punishment at the end of the module. It's not a punitive exercise. It's actually part of the learning process. Building that into our teaching. Not just at the end of the module, which is something that I used to do. So, I'd always do a kind of assignment workshop near the end of the module ... But the recommendations build assessment in right the way through [the semester]. So, week on week, you're talking to students about what they should be doing to work on their assignment and breaking it down, and drip feeding that information*

> week-on-week has made it much more transparent for students, I think. And [it] has made lecturing actually more enjoyable for me, because I can see that it's more enjoyable for them! And they're much less anxious. (Lecturer, Wiseman University)

> I think assessment also felt like: 'Right! The learning process is over and now you're gonna be assessed'. Whereas, actually, what strikes me now, and despite some initial resistance around: 'Oh God, am I spoon feeding them here? You know that initial sort of resistance. But, actually, once they started doing this, I thought, on a purely pragmatic level, hopefully it means better assessments outcomes. In that they aren't way off the mark. But actually, now I increasingly see assessment as part of the wider learning process. (Lecturer, Meadow University)

THE IMPACT OF THE RIPIAG ON STUDENTS *FROM THEIR TEACHERS' PERSPECTIVES*

Staff participants reported that they had noticed clear and positive changes in *all* their students' attitudes and behavioural responses to assessment on modified modules. For example, they reported noticeably higher levels of independence in relation to their students' ability to get on with their assignments without continuous direct intervention from them (as their lecturers). They also noted that conversations about assessments with students on modified modules were less about 'how to do them'? 'What does the lecturer want me to do?' Or 'how to get started?' Students, instead, used these sessions simply to 'touch base' with lecturers, and to 'check in' for confirmation.

They also reported that students on the modified modules generally demonstrated higher levels of understanding of the assessment and of what constituted stronger and weaker pieces of work, why they were and what they looked like. Consequently, participants reported that this translated into much higher levels of confidence among students when approaching their assignments on the modified modules. This was in stark contrast to the lower levels of confidence that they displayed when doing assignments on non-modified modules.

> *I've seen less reliance upon me to give them the answers to how to do this. And that they're more confident in just getting on with the task and with the resources ... There's less questions [on] what are we doing? But it's more: 'This is what I'm doing. And this is what it [the guidance] said to do ... I just want to double check? ... So, now they're almost using me as a kind of [person just for] double checking, and not as the kind of fountain of all assessment knowledge... Particularly when I speak to students or hear students, saying things like: 'I'm happy with this module. I'm happy with this assessment. I'm not worried about this assessment. I'm good for this one.' I've noticed that difference. (Lecturer, University of Bourne)*

> *I think for me, my students have been overwhelmingly positive, and very vocally so ... And even this week, I've done one-to-one tutorials with all my students, and they've all said: 'I'm fine with this assignment. This is the one I feel confident on. This is the one I really understand. I feel like I really know what I'm doing with this one.' And that has been a consistent theme ... The mid-module evaluation has been overwhelmingly positive about how well equipped they feel about the assignment, how much they understand what they've got to do. That it's been made really clear to them ... So, I think, definitely, I've seen it develop their confidence, and, alongside that, their enjoyment of the module and the content as well. So, definitely positive from my experience. (Lecturer, Wiseman University)*

> *Students have been overwhelmingly positive about it. They've got a greater sense of clarity, I think, on the*

modules where these interventions have been introduced. (Lecturer, Meadow University)

... If I could summarise a sentence of student feedback from the module ... it would be: 'I know what I'm doing with this assignment, it's the other one that I'm struggling with' [Or] 'It's the other module that I'm not sure [about]. It's the dissertation that's stressing [me], but I know what I'm doing with this module.' (Lecturer, Wiseman University)

They enjoy their assignments. I think that's the biggest thing and that really speaks to the fact that they seem to feel more safe and secure in what they're doing. (Lecturer, University of Bourne)

Staff also claimed that all students on the modified modules appeared to be much more relaxed and assured about their assignments when compared to their experiences on non-modified modules, which often translated into higher levels of enjoyment of their assessments. Assessment fear was also noticeably lower among this cohort than it was for others. Staff asserted that this was a direct consequence of the RIPIAG and related learning sessions, resources and activities that they had embedded in their modified modules.

I mean, you know, I did tutorials last week, um, all day with them, one-to-one tutorials online. And that came through again, and again, and again. They might have had really specific questions about, you know, I've put this here, is that okay, or I just wanted to check out I've done this all right. But there was nothing... They were all quite short or we'd spend it chatting about how they were getting on generally and their plans when they graduate. Because they were like, I feel good about this one [assignment]. I feel confident on this one ... So, I think anecdotally, definitely less anxiety, less stress. (Lecturer, Wiseman University)

> Well, and this was across the board. This wasn't just for my racialised students. They [all] loved it. They loved having someone who was talking explicitly and regularly about the assignments. Making it very clear to them what it was that I was looking for. When it comes to doing the assignments, like very clear guidance on how to do the assignment. It's been overwhelmingly positive, I would say. (Lecturer, University of Bourne)

Lastly, the final comments below point to the fact that staff felt that working with the resources had ultimately and generally resulted in the production of a better standard of work from all of their students.

> My students performed really well, and again, I've been kind of told off for like marking them [highly]. But that's not my fault! (Lecturer, University of Bourne)

> I find myself having to comment less on things like structure [an area covered in the modified seminar]. Students seem to be sort of saying: 'Right, OK! I know what an introduction is. I know what the main body should kind of do.' ... Before this intervention, I was ... having to comment more on those kinds of basic things like structure, you know. Try and get your introduction to do this. Try and get a paragraph to do that. Whereas now ... I'll find my feedback is more about higher level [issues] than those kinds of basic [things] ... These kinds of things, which were shrouded in mystery. Seemed to be something that all the students are kind of... getting, and putting into their work (Lecturer, University of Bourne)

> [S]o far I'm finding a generally better level of assessment coming in ... You know, we've had a few more firsts ... I would say the general level of even the middling essays, are at least hitting the mark in terms of content. (Lecturer, Meadow University)

SOME CONCLUSIONS

The testimonies from the staff participants indicated that working with the Racially Inclusive Practice in Assessment Guidance Intervention, and attending the training workshops, had a transformative impact on enhancing their understanding of the ways in which racial inequalities manifest in all areas of teaching (their racial literacy) in a way that was constructive and inclusive. They also illustrated that the intervention was highly effective as a tool which improved their understandings of how, where and the range of racial inequities that manifest in HE assessment and related practices, which resulted in clear and tangible changes in their own everyday assessment practice. They also illustrated how the intervention had directly changed their assessment practice and their ability to provide a more racially inclusive environment, which impacted positively on all their students. However, while the section provides empirical data which shines light on the positive impact of the intervention on staff, it does not shed light on the persistence of the RAG in student performance data on the modified modules. Consequently, the concluding chapter that follows provides an expansive discussion, which seeks to make sense of the clear benefits and limitations of the RIPIAG for positive change in the assessment experiences and performances of students of colour in HE.

8

DISCUSSION AND CONCLUDING COMMENTS

In this concluding chapter, I go about the business of providing some answers to the central questions that inspired this monograph. These are: What are the experiences of assessment for British-born undergraduate students of colour compared to White British students? In what ways are these experiences unequal and why? And: What are the measurable quantitative and qualitative effects of making assessment more racially inclusive for (all) undergraduate students and their teachers?

In answering these questions, I also discuss the broader implications of the findings for widening what we know about how race exclusions work in higher education and, importantly, what frontline educators can do to mitigate them. First, however, it is important to draw attention to the ways in which the unequal experiences of assessment for undergraduate students of colour in this book mirrored some of the wider and more general experiences of race in Britain, and how they were at times congruent with the experiences of racially minoritised groups in other White majority nation states.

RACIAL EXCLUSIONS IN BRITAIN AND WHITE WESTERN NATION STATES

In a general sense, this book adds to a body of work which empirically illustrates how racial inequities persist in Britain and in White Western National states, such as the US, despite the introduction of various progressive social and education policies during the second half of the last century and first decades of the current century (see, for example, Meer, 2023; Solomos, 2003). For example, throughout this monograph, we have seen examples of covert, institutional and systemic race-based inequities in HE assessment. Moreover, we have seen how these exclusions continue to be consistent features within assessment practices and outcomes despite the introduction of the Equality Act in 2010 and more recently, the government's decision in 2018 to formally place the responsibility for addressing the race award gap in student outcomes on higher education providers.

In many ways, this picture mirrors a more general experience for British minority ethnic communities in other areas of social life and especially in housing, law and employment. Shankley and Finney (2020), for example, illustrate how current UK housing law, systems and practices continue to disproportionately disadvantage people of colour in the UK. This is despite racial discrimination in housing policy being outlawed in the UK for over half a century (see Campbell, 2016). Drawing parallels between the UK and US in his 2016 article for *The Center for American Progress*, Sam Fulwood III similarly asserts that in spite of the introduction of the 'Fair Housing Act in 1968, which outlawed housing discrimination, subsequent decades of local, state, and federal public policies [have] continued to support' the 'de facto' ghettoisation of African Americans and Lantin X communities in the US.

In both the UK and US context, people of colour continue to experience inequitable outcomes in the criminal justice system as well as receive disproportionate levels of surveillance and heavy-handed policing by the state. In the UK, this situation has maintained and arguably worsened even after the implementation of reforms designed to specifically address institutionally racist practices and policies within the police that were introduced in response to the MacPherson report some 25 years ago (Shankley & Finney, 2020).

A recent Guardian newspaper article found that on average, people of colour in the UK are paid less than equally qualified White colleagues, with Black British employees earning, on average, 5.6% less than White employees when doing the same jobs. Garcia and Duncan (2023) conclude that it will take another 40 years for the pay gap to close at the current rate of progress. Similarly, *The Australian* Newspaper reported that in 2023, minority 'ethnic men' were paid on average '16–20%' less than their 'Anglo' (White)male counterparts. There was as much as a 36% deficit in pay for Australian women of colour when compared to White women in similar roles. This racialised inequity in remuneration has persisted despite the introduction of the Fair Work Act in 2009. Research conducted by Kings College London (2023) highlight that in many White Western economies, when peoples' racial identities are 'visible' in non-anonymised recruitment processes, people of colour suffer significantly lower outcomes when it comes to being shortlisted for interview when compared to similarly qualified White candidates (see also Meer, 2021).

Young people of colour also experience inequitable outcomes and treatment in *compulsory* education in Britain. The most recent government statistics, for example, showed that in 2023, Black and Brown British children under the age of 18 are still more likely to be excluded and less likely to leave with comparable results in their SATs, GCSE and A-level tests when compared to their White peers (GOV.UK, 2023).

Importantly, similarly to other works on race in Britain (see Alexander, 1996; Herbert, 2007; Rollock et al., 2014; Wright, 1992), this book also details how racial exclusions are intersected experiences and not felt uniformly or in a blanket fashion. Uneven access to various forms of cultural and economic capital and resources, for example, means that some racial and ethnic groups across the UK appear to be able to better mitigate some of the processes of racial discrimination and ghettoisation that are present in all areas of social life. This includes health, sport, the education system, law, employment and housing (see ; Andrews & Palmer, 2016; Byrne et al., 2020; Campbell, 2020; Darko, 2021;

Garner, 2009, respectively). With regards to the latter, for example, government statistics showed that in 2019, Pakistani heritage families were the most likely to live in the most deprived 10% of neighborhoods in Britain (31.1%). This was followed by Bangladeshi (19.3%), Dual heritage White/Black Caribbean (17.4%) and Black Other (16.6%). The families least likely to find themselves in this situation were from Indian- (7.6%), Chinese- (8.4%) and White- (9%) heritage backgrounds (see GOV.UK, 2020). Similar patterns are present in the exclusion and award outcomes in compulsory education (GOV.UK, 2023). As I discuss below, the experiences of exclusion in assessment in the HE sector for the students of colour in this study appear to be equally complex and uneven.

IDENTIFYING RACIAL BARRIERS IN ASSESSMENT

I set this monograph the rather ambitious target of answering the following specific research questions: (1) What are the assessment experiences of students of colour in UK HEPs and how might these contribute to or produce wider outcome differences in awards between them and their White peers? (2) Why do certain heritage students, on average, appear to have differing and uneven experiences of inclusion in certain forms of assessment over others? (3) To what extent are issues of accessibility and inclusion in assessment for minority ethnic students, intrinsic to specific assessment types or connected to wider pedagogical practice? Or to the ways in which wider social and cultural factors – and proxies for race – such as socio-economic background, cultural capital, location and so on, intersect, influence and contribute to uneven experiences (and, in turn, performances) of students from specific minority ethnic groups in particular forms of assessment?

In response, the first half of the book examined the unifying and contrasting issues that emerged from the Black, South Asian and White student participants' stories of assessment within and across subject disciplines. More than anything else, the data here illustrated that there are no simple or essentialised connections between skin colour and assessment performances or preferences. For example, in

Chapter 2, we saw how White Science, Technology, Engineering and Mathematics (STEM) students preferred exams and White sociology students preferred essays. This was largely repeated in the accounts of Black students in Chapter 3, whereby, Black sociology students showed a preference for essays, and Black law and STEM-based students preferred exams. There were also intra-ethnic differences within disciplines along the axis of ethnicity and religion, whereby, some British South Asian students of the Islamic faith were apprehensive about assessments where they were visible, while South Asian undergrads of the Hindu and Sikh faith appeared not to exhibit these kinds of concerns for this mode of assessment.

Above all else, the participants' sometimes messy and, at times, seemingly conflicting stories of assessment make it abundantly clear that the relationships between race, ethnicity and assessment preferences, performances and outcomes are subtle and complex. Racial exclusions and barriers manifest in different aspects of the assessment process, which intersect and translate into uneven and unequal levels of access, performance and awards for students from different minority ethnic groups. This was especially visible across their experiences of pre-assessment support and post-assessment support.

Students' explanations for their assessment preference showed how enjoyment can be a useful, albeit somewhat overlooked and too frequently dismissed, indicator for gauging their ability to access assessment (and curricula more widely). For example, British South Asian Indian and British White students' enjoyment of, and in turn preferences for, certain forms of assessment appeared to be more connected to issues of pedagogy. While for British South Asian students of the Islamic faith and British Black students, enjoyment of certain assessment types appeared to *also* be more directly connected to issues of access and a sense of security when taking them.

These stories of access- and exclusion-related enjoyment also provided an insight into the ways in which assessment and related practices in UK HEPs were often constructed around very specific (White) race and (middle) classed fantasies and expectations of what constitutes a typical university student that were held by education gatekeepers (Campbell et al., 2021). The evidence indicates that students whose race and/or classed biographies, experiences, currencies and capitals fall outside of this narrow frame are not 'meaningfully accounted' for or included within general 'assessment and related activities, policy, practice or support provisions' across the sector (Campbell, 2022, p. 13). An example of this situation in everyday assessment practice and processes in higher education was neatly summarised in the following lengthy account from one University of Bourne academic, who explained:

> *The assumptions of what students can and can't do. What kind of currencies and capitals they bring ... The kind of support available in assessment. The kind of feedback in assessment. How all of these kinds of things ... make the process of navigating assessment much easier for you know, for White-[heritage] students. And this isn't something that comes out of ... some inherent link to their skin colour. It comes from when we think about the kinds of independent activities that students have to do in preparation for the assessment ... Which students are gonna have the time to do this? Just take, for example [when we often hear]: 'if you don't come to class, then you're not gonna get all the information on the assessment.' Well, OK. What students are gonna be those that are most likely to be travelling? What students are gonna be most likely to be those that have care responsibilities? What students and those that are likely to kind of have all those other social conditions that make attendance difficult? ... So, you know all of these processes effect students of colour in assessment.*

This situation also means that the expectations of assessment and related practice are often alien and out of reach for many students of colour. This is especially the case for those who are the first in their family to attend HE and/or from socio-economically challenging locales. Statistically, these are most likely to be young people from British Bangladeshi and/or British Caribbean households (Ellis-Haque, 2023). Put simply, we have seen how in a

HE-system that routinely fails to make assessment success transparent, and without access to the kin- and social-networks that provide alternative avenues to access the information required for assessment success that is more readily available to many of their White and/or middle-class peers, many working-class students of colour are limited in their ability to successfully navigate assessment. When it comes to assessment, they are less likely to arrive in HE with the knowledge of when to start, what to do, how to do it, and how to do it well. We have also seen how the general lack of transparency that characterises assessment in HE has a direct correlation with lower levels of enjoyment and higher levels of exam anxiety and, in turn, mental ill-health experienced by students of colour (Boustani, 2023).

Nicola Rollock et al. (2015) and Derron Wallace (2019) have both demonstrated how Black and middle-class school children are often able to operationalise their parents' cultural knowledge, familiarity with the education system and their wider middle-class currencies, to successfully navigate compulsory education in a way that their working-class Black peers could not. Similarly, to the Black and working-class school-aged students in Wallace's study, the undergraduate students of colour from working-class backgrounds here were also less likely to have access to the currencies or social and kin resources to draw upon to fill the gaps in the assessment provision offered by their HEPs. Against this, the RIPIAG was developed to help make this often otherwise class concealed knowledge transparent, and something that should be taught as part of the content in each module that students take while studying at HE. The effects of evolving assessment practice in this way were transformative for the students and staff participants in this case study.

A BLUEPRINT FOR MAKING ASSESSMENT MEASURABLY MORE RACIALLY INCLUSIVE

How did the Racially Inclusive Practice in Assessment Guidance Intervention improve students from minority ethnic backgrounds' lived experiences of assessment? How did it enhance teaching staffs' ability to understand and navigate the racial inequities that were manifest in assessment? The second half of the book showed that the RIPIAG is the first intervention to directly and empirically *reduce* the race award gap in assessment outcomes between White students and students of colour across the three UK HEPs (at the time of writing). It was also highly effective at enhancing staffs' racial literacy and their students' qualitative experiences of assessment. However, before we discuss and conceptualise these successes in greater detail, it is important to first sketch out the limitations and boundaries of the RIPIAG (and arguably for all interventions that are solely focused on addressing racial inequities manifest in modules or at the module level, more widely).

In 2018 the Office for Students (OFS) placed the responsibility for monitoring and addressing the RAG in student degree outcomes within the Access and Participation Plan (APP) framework. This prompted the launch of a plethora of decolonising and racial inclusion curricula activities/interventions across the sector. This was largely informed by the prevailing academic assumption that there exists a direct causal link between assessment performance and curriculum content (see for example TASO, 2022b).

Despite this flurry of activity, there has been relatively little consistent or meaningful reduction in the RAG. In some instances, the gap has widened for students from specific minority ethnic communities, such as those who self-define as Black British and British Bangladeshi (Douglas Oloyede et al., 2021). Half a decade on from universities taking formal responsibility for reducing the RAG, the sector remains unclear as to the causes of this particular manifestation of race-based inequity and, importantly, what works with regards to mitigating its uneven impact on students of colour.

Sabri (2023) argues that this situation is partly due to the overly narrow and simplistic ways in which HEPs have tended to frame, conceptualise and approach RAGs. She elucidates that the knock-on-effect of this is that the metrics and methodologies employed by HEPs are often too narrow in their scope and sophistication to adequately identify and account for the full range of variables that contribute to the RAG. Put simply, existing ideas and approaches for eliminating the RAG have thus far been too reductive and narrow. They lack a sufficiently intersectional framework to allow us to see and tackle RAGs holistically and in a way that can account for the internal (organisational) and external (societal), as well as cultural, structural and inter-racial barriers that contribute to the inequities in the degree outcomes experienced by students of colour in UK HEPs.

Additionally, RAGs are too frequently 'thought of' as unintended and *un*conscious consequences of policy, practice or individuals, respectively. Of course, this can be true. However, RAGs are also manifestations of colonial processes and cultures that explicitly seek to maintain and reproduce the kinds of race, gender, class and ablism hegemonies that characterise all areas and levels of the academe (Archer & Francis, 2007). The consequence of employing interventions and metrics based on the former ontological position is that they are unable to see or account for *all* of the factors that can contribute to the production of RAGs. These include, but are not limited to, the institutional and *conscious* racial biases that are deeply embedded within the structures and cultures of UK universities that actively work against race equity work and interventions (I discuss these in more detail in the Afterword).

Clearly, RAGs are complex and the sum mosaic of multiple layers of overlapping systemic, social, economic and cultural racisms. Importantly, the data in this book have shown that they are not the result of barriers solely located in one site, process or area of education, such as the curricula, unconscious biases or assessment. The RAG is one outcome of the interconnectedness of racial barriers and inequities that are present in all of these spaces. This reality has led some anti-racism scholars such as, Ugiagbe-Green and Ernsting (2022), to describe RAGs as a 'wicked problem', which has 'no determinable stopping point'.

This context is useful for understanding the scope and limitations of the efficacy of the RIPIAG for *eliminating* the RAG in its entirety. For example, the intervention's influence does not extend to tackle structural level race-based inequities that can manifest in assessment quality processes, such as those within moderation. Nor does it provide solutions to the influence of a Whitened and Eurocentric curricula (see Campbell et al., 2022), or mitigate the effects of the imbalance in representation between diverse student bodies and Whitened academic faculties, on the assessment performance of students of colour.

The scope of the intervention extends only to its ability to (1) enable staff to address the exclusions experienced by students of colour caused by the pedagogy and practice of assessment at the module level, and (2) to enhance teaching practitioners' ability to see and identify the racial inequities within their assessment practice and make meaningful changes in the module(s) that they convene.

Within this specific context, the second half of the book showed some of the ways in which the intervention was highly effective for achieving measurable, meaningful and positive change in relation to enhancing staff understandings of race inequity in assessment, and to enhancing students' experiences of assessment and outcomes.

MAKING MEASURABLE IMPROVEMENTS TO THE RACIAL LITERACY AND RACIALLY INCLUSIVE PRACTICE OF LECTURING STAFF

In his study on White secondary school teachers, Joseph-Salisbury (2020) argued that improving the racial literacy of typically White and non-race specialist staff was crucial for making compulsory education spaces more inclusive for Black and mixed-race students (See also Morgan & Lambert, 2023; Saleh, 2023). His point is apt here in a general sense. Module convenors in higher education and their familiarity with – and understandings of – race-based inequities in their assessment practice, or lack of, also had a direct impact on their students' ability to access, engage and succeed in their assessments. Since 2018, faculties in HEPs that predominantly consist of academics who are White and unfamiliar with issues of race in education, have been increasingly asked by their institutions to decolonise their content and practice. However, seldom have institutions provided training or explicit guidance on what this instruction looks like in practice. This general situation left most of the non-race specialist staff in our study to have to work out how to do this for themselves. This often meant drawing on what they described as their own 'hazy', and often speculative, understandings of what decolonising is and what decolonising action looks like.

In Chapter 7, we saw how prior to engaging with the RIPIAG, the practitioners' understandings of what 'decolonising' their practice meant was almost exclusively centred on pluralising the existing knowledge within their taught curricula. As we might expect, their views rehearsed existing dominant decolonising discourses.

Informed by a combination of work conducted by Equity, Diversity and Inclusion, race, anti-racism and decolonial scholarship, the majority of the current decolonising higher education conversations across disciplines has thus far been almost entirely focused on disrupting and pluralising the White and Eurocentric canon and perspectives that shape the academe, its outputs and what is considered valuable knowledge, voices and thought (Akel, 2020). The Keele University 'Decolonizing the Curriculum Network' definition for the aims, objectives and purpose of the 'decolonising' project provides a useful illustration of the current orthodoxy.

> *Decolonization involves identifying colonial systems, structures and relationships, and working to challenge those systems. It is not 'integration' or simply the token inclusion of the intellectual achievements of non-white cultures. Rather, it involves a paradigm shift from a culture of exclusion and denial to the making of space for other political philosophies and knowledge systems. It's a culture shift to think more widely about why common knowledge is what it is, and in doing so adjusting cultural perceptions and power relations in real and significant ways. (Cited in Campbell et al., 2021, p. 32)*

Despite a recognition that decolonising education should address all forms of colonial processes manifest within the sub-cultural world of the academe, the majority of the existing canon has generally been focused on disrupting and dismantling a 'Eurocentric curriculum' that 'perpetuates White privilege and Western Knowledge' (Takhar, 2023, p. 2).

This academic consensus view, alongside a general and sector wide absence of guidance on what decolonising looks like in practice, appears to have inadvertently resulted in the current situation described above. Whereby, for the participants in this study, the decolonising education conversation appeared to start and stop with a conceptual, theoretical and philosophical debate.

This was arguably most apparent when staff participants were asked the routine question: 'What does decolonising education mean to you?' All of their answers coalesced around words and terms such as 'disruption' of certain 'knowledges' 'histories', 'powers', 'privileges' and 'curricula'. More interestingly still, was the fact that despite each participant being interviewed separately, all rehearsed almost verbatim what we might describe as this (fairly recent) decolonising orthodoxy (discussed above).

In Chapter 7, we also saw how participants were often unable to consider or speculate about how colonial processes might operate in other areas of education that existed outside of the curriculum. This was especially noticeable when they were asked: 'What do you think we mean by, and how might we begin to, decolonise assessment?' To which no one had a clear or direct answer. Put simply, staff were able to imagine and reproduce the dominant decolonising discourse in relation to curricula, but struggled to apply the decolonising conversation to their practice if related to areas that were *beyond* the curriculum.

The difficulties experienced by staff described here raise important questions about how helpful the current decolonising conversation and frame is as a practical pedagogy for non-race specialists who want to make their practice more equitable, if it does not also contain clear blueprints for enacting racial inclusion action. Moreover, the almost laser-like focus on the curriculum appears to have potentially and inadvertently constrained staffs' ability to imagine or consider the full range of colonial processes that are in operation within their practice and classrooms. Against this situation, a combination of working directly with the RIPIAG, and through the lens of *racial inclusion* more widely, appeared to enhance staffs' ability to imagine and see additional sites of racial violence in and beyond curriculum content. It also helped them to imagine how colonial inequities manifest in assessment.

Exploring assessment through the lens of race inclusion appeared to also open their thinking up to a much broader conversation and recognition of the ways in which colonial apparatuses and processes within their assessment practice marginalise students of colour. Importantly, this lens moved participants' thinking on from only being able to repeat existing orthodoxies, to taking transformative action that, in turn, made assessment in their modules more accessible, equitable and enjoyable for the students of colour on their programmes.

For example, Chapter 7 illustrated how the RIPIAG fostered a greater understanding of the complex and multiple ways in which the assessment successes and grade outcomes of students of colour are often predicated on various social and cultural currencies that certain raced groups are more or less likely to possess. We also saw that it enabled staff participants to move beyond perceiving race-inclusion in assessment as an amorphous concept, and towards actionable changes in their practice, which resulted in a noteworthy enhancement in their students' competencies, attitudes, experience and performances in assessment on modified modules, as well as a reduction in the levels of exam stress reported by their students.

In sum, exploring racial barriers through the lens of decolonising often stifled the conversation as much as helped it. By contrast, exploring this through the lens of racial inclusion seemed to be more helpful in relation to helping educators think more broadly and beyond curricula, to include assessment and related processes and also for helping them to generate practical solutions for these barriers in their practice.

THE IMPACT OF MAKING ASSESSMENT RACIALLY INCLUSIVE *FOR ALL STUDENTS*

The positive impact of the RIPIAG intervention on their pupils' assessment experiences reported by staff corroborated with the performance data of students on treated modules explored in Chapter 6. The quantitative data showed a consistent reduction in the RAG in student assessment performances at the module level. This reduction was apparent in the modified modules when tested against the assessment performances of students on previous non-modified iterations of each module, the aggregate score of all other non-modified modules at that level and against the national average.

The positive impact of the RIPIAG resources was further corroborated by the qualitative accounts taken from students on the treated modules. Their testimonies showed how the intervention was almost universally effective for improving Black, South Asian and White students' comprehension of what was required in all aspects of the assessment process. For example, the Critical Assessment Schedule enhanced students from all backgrounds' familiarity with, and comprehensions of, the assessment journey. The Critical Assignment Brief improved students' ability to deconstruct verbose assignment questions into shorter and more manageable sub-questions. The Modified Seminar Workshops enhanced students' ability to breakdown the assignment from a large and daunting undertaking, into a set of smaller and more manageable sub-activities. The Active Group Marking Exercises had high efficacy for developing Black, South Asian and White students' comprehension of how the deconstructed aspects of the assignment joined together to form a coherent narrative in a full assignment. Put another way, the RIPIAG *was effective* at enhancing students from all three raced groups' understandings of when to start, what to do, how to do it and what assessment success looked like.

The RIPIAG had a transformative impact on reducing the levels of stress and anxiety that accompanied assessment. The intervention also facilitated the construction of a pedagogical environment in which students felt safe and confident to be innovative and to show wider thinking on their assignments in modified modules than they did on assignments in non-modified modules.

There were also noteworthy differences in the experiences of students of colour on treated modules when contrasted with the experiences of students of colour on non-treated modules, and between them and their White peers. To recap, in Part 1, we saw that a lack of active pre-assessment support in module content meant that students were often left with only a partial understanding of the marking process, scheme and how assignments were scored. This general lack of assessment transparency meant that Black and South Asian students of the Islamic faith in particular, like all students, were often left to speculate the reasons when grade outcomes did not correspond or reflect the effort they had invested into their assignments. However, for students from these two backgrounds in particular, who are more likely to experience systemic and everyday racism in the UK, 'anomalies in grade outcomes were understood as simply being another example of the inequalities that they had to endure in UK education systems and in a British society, which is routinely and systematically hostile to them' (Campbell, 2022, pp. 7–8). In the absence of being meaningfully taught how grades were assessed, when submitting their assignments, students of colour who were surveyed in Part 1, could only 'pray' that the person marking their work was not a racist if they wanted 'to do well' (Campbell, 2022).

Secondly, Chapters 2, 3, 4 and 5 indicated that the Black and South Asian experiences in assessment were characterised by lower levels of entitlement when compared to White peers. This resulted in a higher sense of underserved-ness among students from these backgrounds compared to White peers. This was especially the case when it came to requesting or approaching staff for additional assessment support or clarity. They were also more likely to be concerned about the potential negative consequences that asking for help might have on their lecturer's perceptions of their intellect – or lack of. The resultant unwillingness to expose themselves in this way stemmed from a 'racialised habitus', which instills within many students of colour a reluctance to approach staff as a form of psychological racial self-preservation (Singh et al., 2022).

By contrast, the accounts of students from these minority ethnic backgrounds on treated modules, in Part 2, showed that the increase in transparency of the assessment process, directly brought about by the intervention, meant that Black and South Asian students better understood how they were being assessed and what was required to achieve desired grades, when compared to their peers on other modules. One direct consequence of this was that participants of colour here no longer needed to resort to 'praying' that their marker did not harbour racial biases (which is not to say that this exercise eliminates the possibility of students having a 'racist' marker). It also meant that they had a better understanding of their assessment and thus did not need to expose themselves to their lecturer to be able to complete the task *if they did not feel comfortable doing so*.

The assessment experiences of Black students particularly highlighted the 'wicked' nature of RAGs (Ugiagbe-Green & Ernsting, 2022), and demonstrated some of the limitations when employing pedagogy focused interventions as the sole response to addressing the RAG. In Chapter 6, for example, disaggregated quantitative data indicated that while the aggregate RAG had shrunk between all students of colour and White peers on treated modules, Black students continued to experience the widest RAGs when compared to all other groups. This was corroborated by the Black student testimonies explored in Chapters 3 and 6, which shone light on the multiplicity of challenges and barriers to achieving outcome parity in assessment that were uniquely faced by Black students *within* and *outside* of the assessment process. They reminded us, for example, that students from this minority ethnic background are the most likely to need to find additional income to support their studies and are most likely to need to commute to campus (both impacts negatively on attendance). This is in addition to the fact that African- and African-Caribbean heritage students are also statistically more likely to live in socio-economically challenged locales, be the first in their family to go university or to have received a state-education, especially when compared to East Asian, South Asian Indian and White British heritage peers (Byrne et al., 2020). They are also most likely to face micro-aggressions and overt and structural forms of discrimination in- and outside of the academe (Butler, 2023). They are also more likely to feel lower levels of belonging and higher levels of alienation in HE, have fewer role models in their faculties that look like them, have a less positive experience of Student Wellbeing Services and Personal Tutor support and are at a greater risk of experiencing mental ill health than their peers (Douglas Oloyede et al., 2021).

This backcloth of systemic, social, cultural, psychological, economic, and structural race-based barriers impacts negatively on the assessment performances of Black-heritage students and on their ability to achieve outcome parity with students from other race and ethnic groups, who are less likely to face these challenges or to face them in the same – or in such acute ways. This may go some way to understanding why, despite the universal and positive impact of the intervention across all of our student participants in this case study, its ability to ensure parity in award outcomes is buffered by the fact that students from different raced and ethnic backgrounds do not start from the same position in relation to the challenges that they face outside and *inside* the academe.

Clearly, race is a proxy for wider social inequities, which are more salient in specific social and educative contexts and more acute for students from different backgrounds. The data presented in this book shows that the Racially Inclusive Practice in Assessment Guidance Intervention can mitigate against many of the specific raced barriers and inequities that exist *in* assessment practice. However, it also highlights the intervention's limitations with regards to its ability to mitigate against the wider and specific anti-Black barriers and inequities within HE (and wider social life in the UK) that specifically stymie Black students from achieving grade outcome parity with other raced students and White peers. They remind us that there is no simple or singular remedy for RAGs.

Final Thoughts

This book is the first case study to provide empirical data which sketches out the ways in which assessment works unevenly for students of colour, why this happens and what we can do to measurably mitigate these exclusions. In doing so, it provides the academe in the UK and higher education sectors across White Western nation states more widely, with a much-needed starting point for a new and empirically driven discussion on race and assessment.

At its most rudimental, this book has empirically demonstrated some of the ways in which assessment is a process which contributes to the marginalisation of undergraduate students who are from racial minority and working-class backgrounds in the UK. Against this reality, the positive and measurable impact of the intervention documented throughout is clear. It has high efficacy for improving the assessment experiences of *all students*, and especially students of colour. It is the first recorded intervention to directly contribute to a *reduction* in RAGs in UK HEPs. However, it is also clear that it cannot *eliminate* them on its own. The data here suggests that to eliminate the RAG requires a suite of interventions designed to forensically target the different and various social, structural and pedagogical barriers in assessment and within racially minoritised students' wider HE experiences that all contribute to RAGs. The take-away message is loud and clear. It is only through a forensic and co-ordinated approach, that addresses each thread of the race-inequity mosaic that underpins the RAG, that this challenge will cease to be a 'wicked' problem.

AFTERWORD: 12 YEARS A BLACK RACE INCLUSION ACADEMIC – SOME REFLECTIONS ON WORKING IN A *'POSTRACISM'* SPACE

By the time you read this, it will be (at least) my 12th year in a permanent contract as a full-time senior scholar of race and inclusion. So, what has changed in relation to race inclusion in HE and in Britain during this time, and what has stayed the same? How and what conceptual frames have scholars employed to make sense of this drama? Are existing ways of understanding questions of race, inclusion, race *and* inclusion, and *resistances* to race inclusion in the academe still relevant and helpful? Drawing on some of my own experiences as a British-born Black man whose career as a senior academic and leader in the academe spans across the last two decades, this afterword concludes this monograph with some reflections on these questions.

RACE AND PROGRESS IN BRITAIN IN THE NEW CENTURY – A PARADOX?

In a recent *Talking Race* podcast, the eminent Professor of Sociology, Les Back, described professional football in this third decade of the 21st century as a racially 'paradoxical' space because it is characterised by salient examples of both inclusion and exclusion, progress and status quo maintenance, and, even in some cases, perceptions of social regression by some players of colour. He evidences his assertion by highlighting how professional football in the UK today is a space where Black footballers, such as Raheem Sterling, can speak openly and candidly about the ways in which they experience structural exclusions in post-playing opportunities for coaching and management (see Burdsey, 2022). Or take part in anti-racism activism, such as the social media 'blackout' organised in the Spring of 2021, which was in response to the abuse that Black players routinely receive on social media. Moreover, Black and dual-heritage male players who represent the national team are now encouraged by their White teammates, coaches, union and governing body, the FA, to leave the field of play during matches *if* or *when* they receive racial abuse from opposing supporters or players.

Back concluded that all this was seismically different to the Black experience in professional football during the last decades of the last century. This was a time when Black professional footballers, like the late Cyril Regis, were routinely subjected to racist abuse from their own and opposing coaches, players and fans. One might conclude then that professional football today is a far cry from what Jacobs (2023) described as the 'dark old days' of the game, during the 1970s and 80s.

Unfortunately, this view is not altogether accurate. The same Black players who today are celebrated by thousands of supporters were also subjected to something of a backlash from sections of predominantly White soccer fans who took to booing teams who decided to 'take the knee' to highlight the continuing racial inequalities in football and wider society, in the days and months that followed George Floyd's murder by the police in the US. In what can only be seen as a direct rebuttal to soccer professionals expressing their own 'Black Lives Matter' anti-racism activism in stadia across the country, some fans disingenuously claimed that activism which is focused on the plight of one raced group was itself racist, because *all lives (should) matter* equally. In the British Northwest, some football fans went even further and flew a banner over a televised match at Turf Moor Football Ground, which read: *White Lives Matter Burnley!*

The racial abuse directed to Black England footballers Buyaka Sako, Jaden Sancho and Marcus Rashford the following season by their own fans, for missing their spot kicks in the penalty shootout in England's defeat to Italy in the final of the Euro 2020 tournament, served as a stark reminder that Black inclusion in professional football in England today is precarious and seemingly granted on the condition that players of colour must always exceed the expectations that are placed on their White peers to be accepted as sporting equals.

Similar 'paradoxical' stories of racial exclusion and inclusion characterise the minority ethnic experience in contemporary Britain more widely. Since 2000, we have witnessed a dual-heritage Princess in Meghan Markle and the appointment of four British people of Indian and Pakistani heritage as Prime Minister (Rishi Sunak), Home Secretary (Suella Braverman), Mayor of London (Sadiq Khan) and leader of the Scottish National Party (Humza Yousaf), respectively. This is in addition to the UK boasting its most racially (even if not ideologically) diverse front bench in its history. For some, these kinds of markers signal a progressive and even 'post-racial' Britain that is finally at ease with the racial plurality of its population (Miri Song, 2015). This claim was echoed in the Tory Government's recently commissioned report on *Race and Ethnic Disparities* (Sewell et al., 2021), which concluded that race is no longer an impediment to equal access to opportunity or resource in Britain *today*.

This progress is juxtaposed with the fact that this is the same (racially diverse) government that implemented its own version of the hostile environment strategy, which led to thousands of elderly Black Britons being unlawfully deported to 'far off' islands in the Caribbean, with almost all having no living memory of ever residing there. This policy was enacted despite the government's own impact study pre-warning that it would impact unevenly and most painfully on its British citizens from the old Commonwealth. It is also a government that has publicly denied the existence of structural and institutional forms of racism and continues to double down on this assertion even after they were made visible by the Covid-19 pandemic, which impacted most severely on Britain's communities of colour in every measurable way when compared to its impact on White Britain (Campbell, 2021).

This is also against a more general experience of racism in Britain, which includes children of colour being three-times more likely to be tasered by police when committing the same crimes as White young people (Busby, 2020) and Black men being seven-times more likely to die in police custody (Dodd, 2023). Black women today are four-times more likely to die during childbirth (Darko, 2021). According to GOV.UK (2020), British South Asian Bangladesh, Pakistani and Black Caribbean households still overwhelmingly occupy Britain's poorest neighbourhoods, when compared to other communities.

During a keynote lecture that I gave to the *British Society for Sports Historians* in 2018, many of these seemingly antithetical experiences of both exclusion and inclusion for Britain's communities of colour led me to the same conclusion that Les Back would eventually reach some 5 years later – that the experience of people of colour 'in the UK today, [i]s one … of being simultaneously marginalised and included, of being both citizen *and alien*'.

SOME EXAMPLES OF WHAT IT'S LIKE BEING A RACE INCLUSION LEADER IN HE, WHO IS ALSO A PERSON OF COLOUR, IN THE 21ST CENTURY: HAVE WE EVER HAD IT SO 'GOOD'?

In many ways, education and HE are a microcosm of wider society in the UK. My own experiences are full of my own examples of racial equity and inequity in the academe. In Chapter 1, I explained that when I returned to education in 2003, nothing much appeared to have changed in relation to the general Whiteness of my faculty and curricula. But, if my own experiences were to be a barometer, then by the time I submitted my PhD in 2012, it seemed that things were changing across the sector.

In September 2012, I was one of three people of colour appointed as senior lecturers in a previously all White department and within two years, two more academics of colour had joined the team (although, by this time, two of the original three had left because of a lack of support). I was the first Black 'Head' and Course Director in my second role, and I was the first directly Black

African Caribbean heritage person to be promoted to Associate Professor in the 75-year history of my current department in 2022, and I was my university's inaugural Director of its inclusion institute in 2021.

These local experiences have taken place against the backdrop of significant race inclusion developments. For example, since 2018, universities across the sector have committed more resources than ever before to directly addressing racial inequities in student award outcomes and satisfaction rates. This has happened alongside sector wide attempts to 'decolonise' curricula (Arday & Mirza, 2018), and address race-based inequities in the wider student experience. There have also been more formal attempts to neutralise inequities in the employment, retention and promotion rates for staff of colour when compared to their White colleagues, as part of formal institutional commitments to schemes such as the Race Equality Charter. At the same time, the student body has racially diversified during this period, with domicile students of colour now accounting for 25% of the total student community in the UK and representing as much as 50% of the student body in some universities located in the British South and Midlands regions. To paraphrase the post World War 2, Conservative Prime Minister, Harold MacMillan, developments such as these, could prompt some to ask: Have people of colour in the academe *ever had it so good*?

Despite these markers of progress, I, like many people of colour in academia, continue to (and continuously) experience overt and covert forms of racial hostility, gaslighting and macroaggressions from colleagues and peers – and experience this daily. For example, I remember being invited to a pre-conference drink, and, upon arrival, being promptly asked by one of the White organisers if I was the cab driver (to this day, the individual has still not offered me an apology). In most instances, however, racial discriminations within the academe are seldom so blatant and nor are the strategies employed by staff *to resist progressive change and race equity*.

The following lengthy email correspondence with a senior academic some years ago is perhaps a more helpful and illustrative example of the more subtle, insidious and psychologically triggering forms of this resistance. The context of this example was a routine conversation between a course team about making potential changes to a programme of study. The overwhelming majority of the students on the programme were women, and students of colour accounted for nearly one in every three people. At the time, the degree had only one module explicitly focused on race and only one module explicitly dedicated to gender that was focused on women's perspectives. It is in this context that the following correspondence about introducing a new core module takes place. They began...

> *Dear All*
>
> *Ahead of any discussion regarding [the review of the] the degree please see the 'positive' feedback for the module and my resultant proposition to make it a compulsory module on the degree. This is something that is in keeping with [our] wider University strategies ...*

My response ...

> *Thanks for this...*
>
> *[D]o we know how this positive feedback [for the proposed module] is influenced by raced biographies [?]*
>
> *One point I would like to raise is that the current [internal] evaluation on the [programme] ... indicates a clear and unequivocal desire among all ... students for more explicit race and gender-based modules at levels two and three in addition to these topics explored in other modules.*
>
> *More widely, having more explicit modules on these topics at all levels will also tie into the university's ... and department's core targets ... to have more racially inclusive curricula...*
>
> *Anyway, I'm looking forward to a productive discussion tomorrow)*

They responded ...

Afterword

Hi Paul

... Some question and observations: [sic]

*What about class bibliographies [sic] and **disability biographies**? [their use of bold] Do we have detail on that? Disability with mental health is a key target area on attainment as per the Access and Participation Plan.*

My response ...

... All great questions! It'd be really good to talk in person as email can be so limiting - but I'll try and respond as fully as I can here...

[I a]gree completely. I do not think this is an either or... and would love to see modules on disability and class here too. However, I would suggest that this should certainly not be at the expense of the inclusion of new race and gender-based modules, especially given that eliminating the race award and satisfaction gap is one of the university's key priorities ... at the explicit instruction of [senior leadership]...

Sorry for the long email and really looking forward to touching base.

They responded...

Thanks Paul. No need to extend the discussion on here – however in response to your earlier email a team of us have put together a proposal for an optional gender module that will fit with your suggestion:

***The Lives of Ordinary Males and Masculinities** [I have paraphrased this title]*

[Module synopsis] This module will explore issues of men and masculinities in the context of their everyday lives and practices. The module offers a detailed discussion of the theories of masculinities with a particular focus on ideas of hegemonic masculinity (Connell) and

> *how masculinities are contested as well as how they may be seen as sites of discrimination and patriarchal practices. Aspects of masculinities and male identity, such as employment, fatherhood, leisure and sport, combined with issues of race and ethnicity, are considered critically as intersecting social processes. The module will consider masculinities in a historical, comparative framework and question how masculinities, or understandings of such, have transformed and changed over time. Contemporary notions of 'maleness' will (also) be considered comparatively (e.g. [sic] examining transitions in experiences through a man's life course in different socio-cultural contexts). Another key aspect of the module will be to consider real world challenges and situations that men face in relation to issues of health and illness, as reflected, for example, in the disproportionate male suicide rates. This module will draw upon the gender studies critique of sociology from the 1980s onwards and the rise of men's studies in the US and the UK (such as Jeff Hearn, Michael Kimmel, and David Morgan).*
>
> *We have clear expertise in this field (my Phd and publications [he then lists the names of 3 other members of staff])*
>
> *I will send it [the proposal] over to [the teaching and learning lead to be added to the list of changes for the programme] later.*

I found the response surprising and somewhat perplexing for a number of reasons. Firstly, none of the proposed convenors listed had any expertise in race, Whiteness (as it pertained to the experience of people of colour), or on women of colour, despite the senior academics' claims to the contrary. Moreover, one listed member of staff's recent thesis, and only scholarship to that date, was explicitly on the experience of White working-class *men and their families*. Secondly, only one of the listed convenors was a woman and none had a direct lived experience of race. Lastly, the three key authors listed, whose work was said to be foundational to the module (Jeff Hearn, Michael Kimmel, and David Morgan) had all primarily published on issues relating to White men and had no lived experience of being a woman, a person of colour or a woman of colour. My following response to the last corresponding email was in this context...

> *Thanks ... I might have read it [the module synopsis] wrong, but, I don't think this module responds to the issues raised previously fully...*
>
> *I am just unsure how a module on gender which is centred on (White) men reduces the gender [im]balance (or race [im]balance as none in the team are race or Whiteness specialists) on a degree that is, according to our students at least, predominantly orientated to the stories of White men.*
>
> *I just think for equity and to give everyone a fair chance to respond, I would be more comfortable leaving this and any further actions/correspondence on this issue, to the conversation on Thursday when everyone can contribute.*
>
> *But sure plenty of food for thought and to discuss on Thursday.*☺

They replied ...

> *Hi Paul*
>
> *You wrote: 'desire among all of our students for more explicit race and gender-based modules at levels two and three'. This is a gender based optional module that will engage directly with the debates you have suggested. The 'white men' issue I am afraid is your reading of the proposal and not mine – e.g. [sic] Tommy J Curry [a race specialist and a person of colour, who was not listed in the original*

correspondence or module synopsis] for example is useful in black men's studies and the argument against pathologising, etc. Black men's health is a major issue. Sorry – did I miss something here? Wrong gender? Wrong debates?

I decided not to respond.

The correspondence is instructive. Contained within this one dialogue are myriad examples of different ways in which staff actively, consciously, unconsciously, passively and sometimes aggressively resist strategies for making HE more racially equitable – and which people of colour and people working in race inclusion have to navigate.

I chose this example for two reasons. Firstly, it offers some interesting parallels between the resistances to race equity and anti-racism found in HE and in wider society. This is perhaps most obviously demonstrated in the similarities between the two queries: 'What about class bibliographies [sic] and disability biographies?' in response to attempts to specifically address the race-based inequities in the degree programme; and the: What about 'All Lives Matter' response to the Black Lives Matter anti-racism movement, that sought to address the inequities specifically faced by Black people in 2020, proffered by sections of the British public.

These kinds of queries are often bad faith and disingenuous responses to race inclusion work according to sociologist Ali Meghji. He explains that when people say, 'Black Lives Matter', they are not 'saying that other lives don't matter'. They are simply trying to redress the current reality that is 'Black people across the world are denied' the same rights as everyone else 'by virtue of being Black'. He elucidates that to say 'All Lives Matter' in response offers no credible answers to this original situation, as well as diverting attention away from the urgent and specific violence experience by a particular community (cited in Luxon & Zayed, 2020).

Importantly, the takeaway point here is that race equity is not a zero-sum game. In the correspondence, all parties were aware that the introduction of a new module on women of colour would not be an impediment for the development of other modules that were centred on the experiences of other marginalised groups or intersections. If we employ Meghji's frame, what we see is that when questions such as these are offered as a rebuttal to race inclusion work or activism, they invariably act as an alibi for the historic inaction within the organisation that has underpinned the status quo that marginalises people of colour. By the same token, it also provides a rationale to frustrate and block any future action that is designed to disrupt the prevailing status quo. In this case, to resist diversifying the degree programme with more modules about race and women's lives.

According to Bhopal (2023, p. 122), the employment of the 'What about' response is often a strategic attempt to recentre Whiteness 'in relation to gender or class or any form of inequality that White [academics] have a [more] vested ... interest in addressing' or 'direct' connection to. She elucidates that the natural consequence of this process is to 'decenter' [sic] race from the conversation, which acts to 'remind people of colour that their place' and stories 'are secondary' in the academe (Bhopal, 2023).

The email correspondence also shines light on the widespread prevalence of 'gaslighting' as a form of racial violence in the academe. The Sociologist, Sweet (2019, p. 852), describes gaslighting as 'the mind-manipulating strategies of abusive people, in both politics and interpersonal relationships ... [that] damage victims' sense of reality'. Drawing on her review of discrimination at the Metropolitan Police, Baroness Cassey expands by explaining that gaslighting is a 'denial' tactic that is commonly used when an individual's or group's behaviour is confronted for being discriminatory. It is a reaction that seeks to rewrite an event or incident, and recasts the roles of the abused as abuser, and the abuser as the abused. The abuser denies any knowledge of their wrongdoing and, in turn, claims that any offence is the result of the victim's misinterpretation and not because their action is discriminatory. The natural conclusion is that it is the victim that is the wrong doer by making what is now (re)presented as a spurious and baseless accusation. The denial and rewriting of facts acts as a form of psychological violence, which forces the victim to question their own senses and reality. Indeed, this was apparent in the claim that the proposed module which contained (1) a title and synopsis that explicitly referenced men and masculinity, (2) a synopsis that made no reference to race focused authors, and (3) had a team of academics with no lived experiences of race or racism, and contained no one who had published explicitly on the experiences of people or women of colour, was in fact *not* a module that was predominantly *about* White *men*. That it *was* in fact a module *about feminism, women and race*. Thus, *perceiving* it to be a module that was predominantly about White men was the result of *my* incorrect 'reading of the proposal, and not' the intention of the author. All this illustrates the kinds of insidious hostilities that exist within civil discourse in HE that are endured and navigated by those working in racial inclusion *every day*.

The exchanges contained within the correspondence also prompt us to reflect on some of the ways resistance to race inclusion in the academe has been conceptualised by other race scholars over the last two decades. Gillborn (2006) argues that in White-dominated spaces such as higher education, power is rarely relinquished or shared. Milner (2008) argues that gatekeepers tend to only agree to improve the conditions and experiences of marginalised groups, if such actions benefit or 'converge' with their own interests. The interest convergence frame allows us to make some sense of the ways in which certain university priorities were employed as justification for the changes proposed by the senior academic and why other priorities, such as making curricula more racially inclusive, were dismissed. In this case, it appeared to be only the institutional level polices which converged with the local interests, and reflected the biographies of the gatekeepers at the school level, that were acted upon.

Warikoo (2016), however, might instead describe this as an example of what he defines as 'diversity bargaining'. Whereby, equity and diversity policies are embraced by powerful groups within White majority spaces until the point where the 'contract' impacts negatively on their status quo, or on their exclusive access to certain desirable currencies and opportunities. Once that threshold is crossed, the bargain or 'deal' is off (for a more expansive discussion of this, see Steve Raven's (2022) excellent thesis).

Typically, this threat occurs when diversity policies seek to go beyond surface-level change and propose meaningful and structural change, which disrupts the existing racial, economic, social or cultural powerbase of the dominant group. In this case, where including the student voice moves beyond a tokenistic exercise to something that threatens to bring about measurable and structural change to degree programmes and, in turn, seeks to redistribute the power held over who decides what the curriculum contains and whose stories it centres.

Lastly, the rather peculiar decision to propose a module that explicitly centred the (White) male perspective, as response to student calls for more modules that explicitly explored women's and raced perspectives, draws our attention to Kehinde Andrews' (2023) concept of the Psychosis of Whiteness (we might add masculine psychosis here too). He argues that White people are often unable to imagine practical or conceptual solutions to real world and social challenges, which do not position them and their stories as central.

It is worth reiterating the point that the correspondence used above was just one of numerous examples of resistance to making HE more racially inclusive and of racial discrimination more widely that I have experienced over the last two decades. Such as, being asked by security if I knew where the Course Leader, Dr Paul Campbell was, after they saw me working in my single office which had my name it. Being asked if it was true that Black men are good lovers, by a colleague. Or having to respond to a member of staff on a training event, who confessed that 'the problem is' that 'Black boys from London, just culturally, don't respect White women'. Likewise, having to frequently endure accusations of reverse discrimination, usually by White members of staff, for providing clear strategies for diversify the faculty (notwithstanding the fact that this position assumes that existing processes of recruitment, that 'just happen' to continually reproduce an almost exclusively White faculty, are themselves neutral and non-discriminatory). Or being told by a former British South Asian Indian heritage colleague and friend that racial inequality in the academe only exists because I choose to see it, and not because it exists. They explained that because they do not see the world in 'that way', racism had not affected them. They advised that if I did the same, then 'race' would no longer be a barrier for me or for my career (Interestingly, I never heard them make this claim about class or gender-based inequities that exist in the academe).

The frequency and pervasiveness of these racialised (micro) aggressive interactions alongside, structural issues, such as continuing race-based pay gaps, retention, lack of opportunities at senior leadership and a lack of British-born professors of colour in the UK, have prompted race-based scholars such as Bhopal (2018), to conclude that racial inclusion and progress within HE is *not a paradox*. It is an illusion (see also Bhopal 2022).

The perception of HE as a space where people of colour are included is an illusion, or one where people of colour are excluded, or one which is racially paradoxical, are all based on the premise of inclusion and exclusion as fixed and mutually exclusive points. This is arguably too deterministic a view. The sub-cultures and structures which shape contemporary educational spaces in Britain are complex and seldom so definitively one dimensional.

The problem is that the perspective from either fixed point fails to account for, ignores or overlooks the legitimate race inclusion developments that have characterised the last decade; or it (dis)misses the continuing systemic, cultural and institutional race-based barriers that continue to shape the experiences of people of colour in HE. Put simply, an analytical overcommitment to either diametrically opposed position significantly limits the ability to see the possible existence of the other.

Ironically, Bhopal's own diligent work on empirically exposing the limits of the sector's claims to be racially inclusive is a useful example of how universities are spaces where these seemingly diametrically opposed positions seamlessly co-exist. She is a professor who is a woman of colour at an elite Russell Group institution that supports her career and promotes her work, which is ostensibly about how elite Russell Group institutions, including the one where she works, are racially discriminatory, marginalising and where race inclusion is an illusion.

Perhaps the challenge here is in part a conceptual problem that seeks to define racially inclusive or discriminatory spaces as 'total' end points or realities. This is problematic, not least because the academe is the very incubator in which the colonial subject was conceived. It is unlikely then that we will ever get to a point where

HE is fully racially inclusive without tearing it down and building it anew, despite our best efforts (this is an approach that I wholly doubt any sitting Vice Chancellor would support). By the same token, it is unlikely that given the growing inclusion of people of colour in the academe and the economic and commercial value of race equity, that race inclusion progress will not continue to be made, albeit to varying degrees or in ways that might not be entirely satisfying to us who work to this end, or to all the people of colour who constitute the HE space. It appears then that our existing frames for understanding racial equity and in turn 'racism' in HE are not able to capture fully this more nuanced reality. Consequently, I argue that a new kind of *post*racism lens might provide a more helpful way of conceptualising the experience of race in HE in late modern Britain.

POSTRACISM: A 'NEW' CONCEPTUAL FRAME

My use of the term *post*racism is not to be confused with the existing concept of *post*racism or 'post' hyphen 'racism'. These terms (here at least) are typically reference to a society or subcultural space where race is no longer a meaningful factor that facilitates or blocks access, inclusion or opportunities (Song 2015, see also Mukherjee et al., 2019). *Post*racism, as I employ it, is instead a reference to a space where all or any manifestations of racial discriminations and anti-racism seamlessly and simultaneously co-exist, despite their apparently antithetical relationship. It derives from Baudrillard's description of the postmodern period as one which is characterised by the entanglement and implosion of the simulated and the 'real' (Storey, 2001, p. 152).

Drawing on this thesis in an ephemeral way, digital media scholars, such as Kaitlynn Mendes (2023), employ the precursor 'post' in postdigital to signal the erosion and entanglement between peoples' online and offline worlds. She asserts that this conceptual framework moves us beyond the redundant perception of seeing these two worlds as separate, fixed and mutually exclusive points. It allows us to more adequately conceptualise and comprehend how and why for people today, actions in their online worlds have very real consequences in their offline worlds, and vice versa. I similarly employed 'post' to conceptualise *Post*blackness in late modern Britain, 'as a reference to the existence of multiple, contrasting and even conflicting interpretations of [B]lackness', and to 'provide a more analytically and conceptually useful descriptor - and an appropriate starting point for future work in this area' (Campbell, 2016, p. 239).

How then might I summarise the characteristics of HE as a *post*racial space? It is a space where people or a person of colour can be simultaneously hired, promoted, celebrated and supported alongside experiencing race-based structural inequalities, microaggressions and psychological violence – and, even by the same policies, designed to open the space up to them, or by the very same people who claim to be their allies.

It is a sector that signals, and aggressively markets, its diversity credentials. It provides pathways to increase the participation of students of colour in the academe and celebrates the racial diversity of its student body. At the same time, it contains numerous structural barriers that limit those same students' chances of leaving their degrees with equitable outcomes, and cultural forces that limit their chances of having equitable experiences of belonging and satisfaction, as well as social barriers that limit their ability to progress into careers in the academe. As we have seen throughout this book, it is a space that invests significant resources into anti-racism strategies, policies and interventions, but contains constituents who actively resist and work against those strategies from making meaningful change. Nor does it mandate the inclusion of these resources for race inclusion into practice. HE as a *post*racism space is ultimately one where racists and anti-racists existentially and equally 'feel' that the space does not work for them, but always works in the interests of the other.

Importantly, the *post*racism frame does not challenge the value or existence of the theoretical frames explored above, such as the illusion of inclusion, diversity bargaining, interest convergence and so forth. It instead offers a more nuanced conceptual frame, which enables us to better understand how interpersonal, systemic, cultural and institutional attempts to both encourage and stymie racial inclusion within the sector, co-exist simultaneously within single HEPs, schools and departments. To end at the beginning. This frame allows to understand how the race and inclusion paradox is not actually so paradoxical at all.

APPENDIX
'Policy Shorts': Mapping and 'Tackling' Racial Inequities in HE Assessment – Summarising the Case Study

This chapter is explicitly for policymakers, educationalists and anyone else who might not have the time to read this book in its entirety, but, require concise answers to the following questions: What are the inequitable experiences of assessment, especially for students of colour? What practical steps can we take to make assessment more racially inclusive? What are the benefits of making assessment racially inclusive, and for whom? What data do we need to measure the effectiveness of making assessment practice racially inclusive at the modular level? Put simply, the job of this chapter is to provide a series of concise summaries of the key take away points from this work and the resultant recommendations for change. However, this will of course mean that for those of you who have read all of the previous chapters, there will be some repetition here.

Before we begin, it is worth reminding you, the reader, at the outset, that the accounts included in this report are students' own interpretations and perceptions of the educational processes which shape their experiences of assessment. As such, they may not always be an accurate account of these processes. However, where this is the case, it is not simply enough for us to dismiss these moments as inaccurate and thus, not to require our attention or action. Students' perceptions shape their feelings towards, and experiences of, assessment and how they make sense of their university experience more widely. This includes their sense of efficacy for different assessment types, their ability to achieve success and their trust and faith (or lack of) in education as something that works for *or against* them. Consequently, where accounts ring true, we as educationalists should use them to make changes to our practice. Where perceptions appear inaccurate, this often indicates a lack of transparency in our practice and thus, we need to see this as an opportunity to show our students how this is not the case and, ultimately, convince them that this is a space where they are treated equitably in education.

A SUMMARY OF HOW ASSESSMENTS ARE EXPERIENCED DIFFERENTLY BY UNDERGRADUATE STUDENTS FROM SOUTH ASIAN, BLACK AND WHITE RACIAL BACKGROUNDS

Data indicates that relationships between race, ethnicity and assessment preferences, performances, and outcomes are subtle and complex. They manifest in different aspects of the assessment process, which intersect and translate into uneven and unequal levels of access, performance and awards for students from different minority ethnic groups. The following examples illustrate the emergent ways in which race featured in student experiences, in relation to their assessments, across four subject disciplines (biology, physics, law and sociology).

ASSESSMENT PREFERENCES AND ACCESS

In a general sense, participants' preferences for specific forms of assessment appeared to be strongly connected to their perceived ability to be successful in any given assessment type. This was the case across all disciplines. However, there were certain features within different types of assessment that appeared to chime with, put-off, advantage and disadvantage students from particular minority ethnic groups and on certain courses.

Exams

Black, South Asian and White Science, Technology, Engineering and Mathematics (STEM) and law students preferred exams, partly because the 'gap' between the expectations of exam writing at FE and at HE was less pronounced than they were for other assessment types. This familiarity facilitated a clearer understanding of what was required to score well.

The schedule and timetabling of exams (typically at the end of the semester) were also something which was attractive to students across all ethnic groups and disciplines. They asserted that its place in the calendar meant that issues such as when to start preparation and revision were clearly – albeit unintentionally – signposted (this was not the case with coursework, where students claimed that they were often unsure of at what point in the semester to start working on their assignments). This point was especially applicable to the experience of Black and South Asian participants, who are statistically more likely to need to balance assessment preparation with commuting to university from outside of the locality and/or with commitments to work (to supplement the cost of their studies).

By the same token, all STEM and law students expressed an aversion for coursework-based assessments, including lab reports, because they felt that FE had ill-prepared them for these forms of assessment at the undergraduate level. Also, because they considered these types of assessment to be counterintuitive. Coursework and lab reports, for example, were seen to be an inexact science that were subjectively assessed and thus had greater potential for assessor bias. Essay questions frequently required deconstructing. Students felt that all this placed them in greater jeopardy of providing a wrong answer.

While it was not entirely surprising that assessments with more definitive outcomes fitted more easily with the learnt pedagogical dispositions and preferences of natural science-based students, this last point does raise important pedagogical questions around the objective of this type of assessment: Are essays there to test students' ability to work out questions, or an opportunity for students to demonstrate the amount and level of knowledge learnt on a module? If the latter, then much more consideration needs to be given to the clarity of the essay questions that we employ.

Coursework, Essays, Portfolios and Lab Reports

Coursework was the preferred choice of assessment for the majority of Black sociology students in our study, and some White students. In addition to a greater sense of familiarity and confidence with this form of assessment, that was tracible back to their secondary and FE experiences, they argued that coursework gave them the space to fully develop and edit responses over a longer time. This was in direct contrast to their feelings and perceptions of exams, which were seen to be a one chance form of assessment that was equally dependant on their subject knowledge *and* their ability to perform well on the day.

Presentations and Non-anonymised Assessments

Preferences for presentations and other forms of non-anonymised assessments were more overtly split along race and ethnic lines (although it should be remarked that all students expressed a general dislike for group presentations, because grade scores were aggregated across the entire group). Both White students and South Asian students (predominantly of the Hindu or Sikh faith), who enjoyed presentations, appeared to remark solely on the pedagogical advantages of the assessment. Namely, that they could receive instant feedback and show extended knowledge through Q-and-A with the assessor.

However, students who were Black and/or South Asian of the Islamic faith were more likely to be sceptical of all forms of non-anonymised assessments. Importantly, the basis for scepticism was different for students from different minority ethnic backgrounds. This was indicative of the different educational experiences of inclusion borne out from their specific minoritised identities. For example, South Asian biology students of the Islamic faith felt that 'visibility' left them open to ethnic and religious-based anti-education stereotypes and biases, which impacted negatively on their grade outcomes. Black sociology students, however, were concerned that in presentations, grade awards were influenced by their capacity to mask their Blackness, and (re)shape their answers and performances in accordance with White middle-class cultural language and capital. Put simply, they believed that being too Black in the way that they spoke and performed placed them at a disadvantage. In this way, students were conscious of the myriad ways in which their raced identities and cultural values *might* work against them in educational spaces and outcomes – and visibility in assessments limited their capacity to mitigate this reality.

Dissertations and Research Projects

Feelings towards dissertations were ambiguous. On the one hand, all students (that this form of assessment applied to) saw it as a rare opportunity to study an area that was personally, professionally or academically significant to them – and in the case of Black students, this was often, but not always, a project that related to their experiences of race. However, there were noteworthy differences between the experiences of White and Black students when it came to their levels of confidence in the topic-areas that they could examine, finding suitable supervisors, and to achieving higher level grade outcomes. White students were generally confident that all this was available and could be achieved. Conversely, the Black students in our study were much more anxious and sceptical of finding a supervisor who was racially, academically or generally interested in race. This issue was central to their confidence about having a favourable dissertation experience and positive grade outcome.

RACE AND PRE-ASSESSMENT SUPPORT

Importantly, when students arrive at HE, their initial positive or negative performances in assessments reinforce their preferences for certain forms of assessment. Unless dismantled, these constructed efficacies often stay with students and influence their performances in assessment throughout their time in HE.

Pre-assessment guidance and greater familiarity with the marking criteria emerged from the data as a way to directly create positive perceptions of assessment. By the same token, it was also an effective way to breakdown the (pre)existing negative perceptions of assessment that some students (often) held. It was also seen as vital for helping students to learn what constitutes and what is required in assignments that achieve higher level award outcomes. However, the levels of pre-assessment support offered were claimed to be inconsistent across lecturers and modules. In turn, all students called for *more* structured and consistent guidance for all assessment types, and especially during their transitions from FE to HE.

Additionally, students felt that the use of what we might describe as 'passive' modelling exercises was often unhelpful. For example, they spoke of some staff making previous 'good' scripts available in repositories for them to see. However, students pointed out that what made these essays 'good' or 'bad' was not always obvious to them. Instead, they called for more 'hands on' exercises, which made clear what it was that made work successful and how this related to the marking criteria.

The comments from some South Asian students, of the importance of this kind of pre-assessment support, remind us that race and ethnicity are a proxy for wider conditions of social life, which often place students from these backgrounds at a disadvantage in Higher Education Providers (HEPs) and in assessment. In this case, students from minority ethnic backgrounds in the UK are more likely to be the first in their families to attend university. In turn, they indicated that assessment support was even more essential for students from their communities. They said that they were less likely to have kin who had been to university and who could provide them with this kind of help, which plugged any lack of pre-assessment support provided in their modules.

Students' calls for more guidance and standardisation of pre-assessment support is in part connected to the fact that since the mid-2000s, education in most comprehensive and FE institutions has largely embraced pedagogical approaches such as Assessment For Learning (AFL). This approach explicitly illustrates to students what is expected at different levels of work (between an A grade response, B grade response, and so on). The basic tenet of AFL-type models of learning is that for a student to produce higher-level work, they must first know – or be shown – what it looks like. This pedagogical practice is at times juxtaposed to many of the cultural practices within HEPs more generally, which sometimes views attempts to standardise practice and calls for assessment 'modelling' as something which stifles talent, innovation and excellence, instead of supporting, nurturing and facilitating it. Given that this experience is relatable to an increasing number of all of our student population, this is an expectation that must be met.

RACE AND POST-ASSESSMENT SUPPORT

All students reported that written and oral feedback were important for development, but claimed that, in practice, written feedback was often ambiguous, vague and unclear. They claimed it often failed to clearly explain in accessible language what they needed to do to improve, and what this looked like in practice. It also failed to clearly distinguish between structural and stylistic issues or to provide clear explanations for how feedback applies and improves future work.

Students remarked that any such issues with written feedback were often circumvented by face-to-face or oral feedback. This was perceived to be essential, because it provided a platform for students to engage in constructive dialogue with lecturers about their work, explained their received grades, developed their understanding of the assessment and provided useful guidance on future assessments. However, the experience of oral feedback was not universal for all students from all ethnic and cultural backgrounds.

For example, White STEM students felt that oral feedback was a forum where they could openly challenge grade outcomes and question the support offered throughout the module. By contrast, both Black and South Asian students did not report the same levels of confidence in seeking out oral feedback or in engaging in such open dialogue with faculty members.

This one example raises important wider questions that we must address. These include: Does oral feedback work equally for all of our students? Which students may or may not feel entitled or comfortable enough to access oral feedback? Is written feedback effective if it is dependent on oral feedback? It also raises broader questions to do with the accessibility of oral feedback, and whether it should be employed as an essential – and not a supplementary – channel for effective feedback? Importantly, it reveals how the experience of assessment, or aspects of it, can be very different for students from different race and ethnic (and gendered, classed, abled and so on) backgrounds.

RACIALISED DISPARITIES IN ACCESSING CURRICULA AND ITS CONSEQUENCES FOR ASSESSMENT PERFORMANCE AND OUTCOMES

Generally, White students across all focus groups proffered that they were able to easily relate curriculum content, assessments and assessment questions to their own realities and life experiences. This was said to improve their ability to revise, comprehend and conceptualise new theories and for ideas to 'stick'. It was also claimed that it enabled them to more easily work out a question's meaning or enabled them to use their own life experiences to better synthesise or add a critical dimension to their answers – and in turn, produce higher quality responses. This also corresponded with higher levels of students from this group reporting that they enjoyed all forms of assessments more widely.

The lack of a sufficiently diverse or decolonised curriculum and faculty meant it was often difficult for Black students to be able to connect content and assessments directly to their own lived realities. It was argued that to do so would make assessments more enjoyable as well as facilitate more interest in study and foster a deeper understanding and synthesis. In this way, Black students are multiply disadvantaged. Black students have to work harder than their peers to connect with both assessment and curriculum content. It should also be noted that the disadvantage for students of colour

– and the advantage for White students – in this regard was remarked upon by both White students and students of colour.

THE EFFECTS OF A NON-RACIALLY AND NON-ETHNICALLY DIVERSE FACULTY ON ASSESSMENT

Student participants asserted that there is a visible lack of racial and ethnic diversity within faculties when compared to the levels of diversity that exists within the student body. A similar point was made about the relatively low number of staff who are explicitly interested in race (with regards to their expertise). Both points meant that for Black and South Asian students interested studying modules and narratives that directly related to them, or finding a project supervisor who was racially or academically 'aligned' with their research interest, was an opportunity that was predominantly only available to their White peers.

UNEVEN ASSESSMENT SUPPORT AS A FACILITATOR FOR PERCEPTIONS OF HIGHER EDUCATION PROVIDERS AS RACIALLY HOSTILE SPACES

Uneven pre-assessment support, and a lack of opportunities to learn and better understand how assignments were assessed, opened up space for students to speculate about how assessments were assessed and graded. White and non-Muslim South Asian students' speculations here tended to centre on what we might describe as pedagogical-based inconsistencies, subjectivity and biases. Put another way, they claimed that variations in awards given to White students compared to students of colour in assessments, such as coursework, were most likely due to the fact these types of assessment were inexact sciences, and thus more prone to assessor interpretation and subjectivity. However, students who were Black and who were South Asian of the Islamic faith, both tended to speculate that inequities in grade outcomes were likely to be another example of the inequalities that they experience in an education system and society which is routinely and systematically hostile to them. While this may not always be the case, the failure to clearly show what assessments should look like, what constitutes stronger pieces of work and how assignments are assessed, leaves our assessment practices open to these kinds of speculations, especially by students who are rightly wary of being mistreated because of their ethnic identities.

RACIALLY INCLUSIVE ASSESSMENT GUIDANCE

Mapping the race-based barriers experienced by students of colour across social science and STEM-based subjects enabled us to identify pre-assessment support, post-assessment support and barriers directly linked to race as the three main sites of racial violence experienced by students in assessment. This also provided a tri-based framework for change, within which the following *Racially Inclusive Assessment Guidance* recommendations were generated (Campbell et al., 2021):

Recommendations for Pre-Assessment Support

- Introduce signposts in module guides and weekly schedules for when students might begin to prepare for assessments, especially for students at Level 1 and 2. Or consider introducing formative exercises and activities that prompt students to prepare for assessments.

- Introduce more modelling exercises that critically assess examples of previous work.

- Introduce exercises which translate marking criteria jargon into accessible language and provide examples for illustration.

- Introduce more modelling and grading exercises that clearly explain how the marking process works.

- The inclusion of an Assignment Brief, or exercises that 'unpack' essay questions (if the assignment question requires unpacking, perhaps rephrase it to avoid unnecessary confusion).

- Include FAQs, which might include a 'to do list' and a list of common mistakes.

- Introduce more even levels of pre-assessment support for all assessments and across all modules.

- Pre-assessment support should be employed especially during the transition from FE to HE stages. However, it is worth considering employing these support mechanisms during all, and any, transition stages, where expectations of what is required to secure higher level grade outcomes change, even if the mode of assessment does not. For example, changes in what is expected between a first-class essay at Level 1 and at Level 2, and so on.

Recommendations for Post-Assessment Support

- Introduce and improve consistency across the programme on what information is provided and prioritised in written feedback across modules.

- Written feedback should be detailed, concise and avoid jargon.

- Written feedback should provide practical guidance and examples of ways to improve work in future assessments and make distinctions between structural and stylistic issues.

- Written feedback should be clear enough not to require oral feedback to explain or clarify points.

- Oral feedback should be employed as a complimentary mode of feedback.

- Employ a process of making your curricula more racially inclusive (see, for example, Campbell et al., 2022).

Recommendations for addressing race and ethnicity-based obstacles to assessment parity

- Oral feedback should be employed as a complimentary mode of feedback.

- Employ a process of making your curricula more racially inclusive (see, for example, Campbell et al., 2022).

- Introduce more modelling and grading exercises that clearly explain how the marking process works.

- All staff should more aggressively encourage and make clear to undergraduate students that they are interested in, and happy to supervise, projects that are centred on their (students') interests, even if the project falls outside of the staff member's research specialisms.

- Employ assessment modelling exercises of the type outlined above. This will improve transparency of the ways in which students are assessed and reduce suspicions of racial bias in assessment.

- Consider ways to address structural inequalities and lack of diversity in the faculty staffing.

THE RESULTS OF THE *RACIALLY INCLUSIVE PRACTICE IN ASSESSMENT GUIDANCE INTERVENTION* (RIPIAG) FOR MAKING THE EXPERIENCE OF ASSESSMENT EQUITABLE FOR STUDENTS OF COLOUR

The *Racially Inclusive Practice in Assessment Guidance Intervention* (RIPIAG) was developed in the 2021/22 academic year and piloted in six modules across three partner HEPs in the UK and on 175 undergraduate students.

The intervention was developed from the original 8 *Racially Inclusive Assessment Guidance* recommendations for pre-assessment support (listed above). For consistency of application, the pre-assessment recommendations were mined from 8 to 6. These were then developed into the following four teaching resources that constitute the *Racially Inclusive Practice in Assessment Guidance Intervention* (RIPIAG), which staff were required to embed fully into their modules (see Table A1).

Appendix

Table A1. Developmental Process From Racially Inclusive Practice in Assessment Guidance to Racially Inclusive Practice in Assessment Guidance Intervention and Resources.

Racially Inclusive Assessment Guidance: Pre-Assessment Support Recommendations	Racially Inclusive Practice in Assessment Guidance	Racially Inclusive Practice in Assessment Guidance Intervention (RIPIAG)
1: Introduce signposts in module guides and weekly schedules for when students might begin to prepare for assessments, especially for students at Level 1 and 2. Or consider introducing formative exercises and activities that prompt students to prepare for assessments	1: Introduce signposts in module guides and weekly schedules for when students might begin to prepare for assessments, especially for students at Level 1 and 2. Or consider introducing formative exercises and activities that prompt students to prepare for assessments	The Critical Assessment Schedule *This resource relates to Racially Inclusive Practice in Assessment Guidance Recommendation 1.
2: Introduce more modelling exercises that critically assess examples of previous work	2: Introduce exercises which translate marking criteria jargon into accessible language and provide examples for illustration	The Critical Assignment Brief *This resource relates to Racially Inclusive Practice in Assessment Guidance Recommendations 5 and 6.
3: Introduce exercises which translate marking criteria jargon into accessible language and provide examples for illustration	3: Introduce more modelling exercises that critically asses examples of previous work	
4: Introduce more modelling and grading exercises that clearly explain how the marking process works	4: Introduce more modelling and grading exercises that clearly explain how the marking process works	The Modified Seminar Workshop *This resource relates to Racially Inclusive Practice in Assessment Guidance Recommendations 2, 3 and 4.
5: The inclusion of an Assignment Brief, or exercises that 'unpack' essay questions (if the assignment question requires unpacking, perhaps rephrase it to avoid unnecessary confusion)	5: The inclusion of an Assignment Brief, or exercises that 'unpack' essay questions (if the assignment question requires unpacking, perhaps rephrase it to avoid unnecessary confusion)	The Active Group Marking Exercise *This resource relates to Racially Inclusive Practice in Assessment Guidance Recommendations 2, 3 and 4.
6: Include FAQs, which might include a 'to do list' and a list of common mistakes	6: Include FAQs, which might include a 'to do' list and a list of common mistakes	
7: Introduce more even levels of pre-assessment support for all assessments and across all modules		
8: Pre-assessment support should be employed especially during the transition from FE to HE stages. However, it is worth considering employing these support mechanisms during all, and any, transition stages, where expectations of what is required to secure higher level grade outcomes change, even if the mode of assessment does not.		

The Critical Assessment Schedule

The Critical Assessment Schedule (CAS) is a detailed timetable that sets out the key points in the assessment process for each assignment, from start to submission. It includes the exact dates during the semester when students should ideally have started/completed the various tasks (such as, completed an essay plan or produced a first draft of their assignment).

The Critical Assignment Brief

The Critical Assignment Brief (CAB) is a 3-page document (maximum) that contains at least all of the following information:

- Submission Deadline
- Grade Weighting of Assignment
- Assignment Instructions
- Assignment Questions
- Tips and Essential Things to Include (when completing each assignment question)
- Learning Outcomes
- Referencing Instructions
- What is Academic Misconduct?
- Non/Late Submissions

The Modified Active Seminar Workshop

The Modified Active Seminar Workshop (MASW) consists of a series of (inter)active and group-based learning exercises that cover the following areas (at least):

- What do I need to get started?
- Structuring the Assignment

Appendix

- Formulating an Introduction
- Assignment Do's and Don'ts
- Key Advice: What are the differences between stronger and weaker assignments?
- Learning the difference between anecdotal, evidence and critical arguments?

The Active Group Marking Exercise

The Active Group Marking Exercise (AGME) is a group-based activity where students mark previous scripts. Using a combination of the assessment content covered in the MASW and the marking criteria, students have to come to a consensus about the grade score for each script. In each case, they provide a rationale for the awarded grade, using the descriptors in the marking criteria and the lessons learnt in the seminar to justify the grade given. They also have to suggest (at least) one thing that the assignment could do to improve the assignment with an example.

The Racially Inclusive Practice in Assessment Guidance Intervention Training Workshops for Staff

My previous evaluative study on the efficacy of race interventions in education showed that the effectiveness of interventions are often dependent on the extent to which they are fully and consistently embedded into practice by module convenors (see Campbell et al., 2022). To avoid this issue, module convenors were provided with two training workshops and with templates of the four resources to ensure a consistent level of embeddedness of the intervention into their practice across modules.

The remainder of this section reports on the effectiveness of the Racially Inclusive Practice in Assessment Guidance Intervention against the following three tests:

1. Its capacity to improve/develop/progress the levels of racial literacy and understanding of racial inequities in assessment among teaching staff
2. Its capacity to improve students from minority-ethnic backgrounds' experiences of assessment
3. Its capacity to foster a reduction in the race award gap (RAG) in student outcomes in assessment at the modular level

THE EFFICACY OF THE RIPIAG FOR IMPROVING THE LEVELS OF RACIAL LITERACY AMONG HE TEACHERS, STAFF AND LECTURERS

The qualitative data demonstrated that the RIPIAG had a direct, positive and tangible impact on enhancing the racial literacy of participants in a general sense. It was highly effective as a process for advancing teaching practitioners of all raced backgrounds, career stages and disciplines' understandings of how, where and the range of racial inequities that can manifest in HE curricula and related practices.

Exploring racial inequities in education through the frame of 'racial inclusion' instead of 'decolonising' enhanced staffs' ability to think more broadly and outside of the 'box'. It stimulated a broader range of thinking, which enabled lecturers to start to think *beyond* course content as the primary – or sole – site for race exclusion in taught programmes. It also prompted participants to consider how things such as the processes and practices that wrap around their modules are also spaces that can contain specific race-based barriers too.

Working with the intervention directly enhanced teaching participants' ability to identify racial inequities that existed specifically *in assessment*. It helped them to be more aware of the complex and multiple ways in which assessment success and grade outcomes were often predicated on various social and cultural currencies that certain raced groups were more or were less likely to possess. It also improved lecturers' comprehension of how racial exclusions work in their own assessment practice. White staff participants noted that the process was constructive and useful. It was described as a process that made them more aware of their complicity in a system that racially excludes students, in a way that did not make them feel guilty or like they were being attacked.

Working with the RIPIAG helped to plug a general lack of institutional guidance on best race inclusion practice, by providing clear support and instruction that enhanced practitioners' ability to better understand, and rapidly respond to, the racial inequities that manifest in their own assessment practice. It also helped staff be able to move the concept of race inclusion from an amorphous concept to a set of clear actions. This was described by some teaching staff as 'empowering'.

The RIPIAG workshops and training provided were also reported as being especially helpful for enabling staff to translate what was often complicated inclusion discourse into actionable instructions. Lastly, staff participants listed the following positive changes in their students' behaviour, competencies and attitudes in relation to assessment on modified modules:

- Students displayed noticeably higher levels of independence in their ability to 'get on' with their assignments on the modified modules without continuous direct support from lecturers.
- Students on the modified modules demonstrated higher levels of understanding of the assessment and of what constituted stronger and weaker pieces of work, why they were and what they looked like.
- There was a reduction in the levels of stress about assignments reported by students.
- There were noticeable improvements in the quality of their students' work.

THE IMPACT OF THE RIPIAG ON ASSESSMENT PERFORMANCE OF STUDENTS AND ON THE RACE AWARD GAP AT THE MODULE LEVEL

Overall, the quantitative data in our evaluation highlights the RIPIAG's clear and direct capacity to impact positively on reducing the aggregate RAG between students of colour and their White

Table A2. Race Award Gap in Student Assessment Performance on Modified Modules.

University and Module Code	RAG score for Treated Module	Module RAG Average for Previous 2 years	Course RAG at that Level	University RAG
University of Bourne M1	1.25%	6.97%	1.20%	10.0%
University of Bourne M2	1.80%	4.11%	2.85%	10.0%
University of Bourne M3	7.38%	7.63%	−0.30%	10.0%
Meadow University M1	4.70%	30.25%	23.20%	22.0%
Meadow University M2	18.70%	37.0%	20.10%	32.0%
Wiseman University M1	8.0%	10.95%	12.00%	18.6%
Average score	6.97%	16.15%	9.84%	17.1%

peers (see Table A2). The average RAG difference between students of colour and those who defined as White across all treated modules was 6.97%. The narrowest gap reported was 1.25% and the widest 18.7%. In all cases, the RAG on modified modules was below the overall RAG reported at their respective HEPs for 2022, with 83% reporting a RAG difference that was lower than the national average.

We have seen that, in a general sense, the RIPIAG had reduced the RAG between White students and students of colour. However, where recorded, in almost all cases, the RAG for Black students had remained wider than the reductions recorded for all other minority groups. Also, the findings do not account for important anomalies that can all influence the veracity of the quantitative findings here and in future. Nonetheless, the triangulation and repetition of consistent patterns of RAG reduction reported in the performance data from across all the modified modules from different courses, levels and partner HEPs provide the basis for confidence in the Racially Inclusive Practice in Assessment Guidance Intervention's efficacy for reducing the aggregate RAG differential in the assessment performance between undergraduate students of colour and White peers.

THE IMPACT OF THE RIPIAG ON UNDERGRADUATE STUDENTS' LIVED EXPERIENCES OF ASSESSMENT

The testimonies showed that the RIPIAG had a positive and transformative effect on enhancing Black, South Asian and White undergraduate students' levels of assessment literacy and comprehension. It was especially effective at enhancing students from all three raced groups' understandings of when to start, what to do, how to do it and what assessment success looked like.

For example, data showed that the CAS appeared to help students learn the assessment journey. It helped them map when in the semester they should ideally start thinking about their assignment question, when to settle on the question, when to have a first draft complete, and so on. This clarity was transformative for students for whom university and, in turn, assessment at the undergraduate level, were new or alien.

The CAB enhanced all participants' ability to better make sense of their assignment questions and specifically, to be better able to identify exactly what assignments wanted them to address in their responses. Testimonies illustrated how this changed students' overall perceptions of assignment questions from instructions that were unclear and daunting into smaller sub-questions, which were seen to be more straightforward and manageable. Additionally, the CAB reduced the jeopardy that accompanied assignment questions and meant that students were less likely to be faced with the prospect of having to choose between answering questions that they better 'understood' over questions on an area that they were particularly interested in, passionate about or more knowledgeable on.

The MASWs enhanced students' ability to breakdown the total sum assignment into a set of smaller sub-activities. This more deconstructed, scaffolded and modelled approach to completing assignments was considered an essential blueprint for success by students. It was described as an essential 'kit' for 'surviving' the assessment process by some. The exercises within the modified seminars were also transformative in enabling students to better 'see' and learn what assessment terminology *meant and looked like* in their everyday practice and work.

Data indicated that the AGME had high efficacy for developing Black, South Asian and White students' assessment literacy, *from* being able to complete the broken-down and compartmentalised aspects of an assignment (learnt in the MASW) to *comprehending how these dislocated aspects* all joined together to form a coherent narrative in a full assignment. The exercises also directly contributed to improving students' perceptions of their own efficacy to complete their assignment and, importantly, enhanced their confidence of being able to produce higher level responses.

Additionally, accounts from all students and staff showed a direct correlation between the introduction of all four RIPIAG resources and increased levels confidence and lower levels of assessment stress and anxiety in students, when compared to their feelings about their assessments on non-treated modules. For example, their accounts demonstrated how the RIPIAG had directly and successfully transformed students' experiences of assessment from something which was 'individual' to one which was social and dialogic. Student participants asserted that they felt significantly higher levels of *comfort* and *confidence* in their assessments when assessment literacy was learnt through this more dialogic and social learning approach when compared to learning it through the more didactic and individualised lecture style approach that was often employed on other modules.

Inter-marker variables were another significant cause of stress and anxiety in assessments reported by all students. The RIPIAG enhanced students' ability to better understand the module-specific expectations of the assignment tasks. This facilitated a more clear-eyed understanding of what constituted work in each grade boundary and how they were marked in that specific module. All this served to mitigate against inter-marker variables and reduce levels of stress caused by this issue.

Overall, data demonstrated that the four resources which constituted the RIPIAG were all successful in making the parameters of the assignment more transparent for students. This appeared to directly reduce students' levels of anxiety and fear of including or discussing the 'wrong thing' or going 'off topic' in their assignments. Equally important was that this served to *enhance students' confidence to be even more creative* within the confines of the assignment *instead of stifling it*.

DIRECT AND MEASURABLE IMPROVEMENTS IN THE LIVED AND EVERYDAY ASSESSMENT EXPERIENCES OF STUDENTS OF COLOUR

Data demonstrates that the increased levels of assessment transparency and, consequently, enhanced levels of assessment literacy brought about their engagement with the RIPIAG. This meant that students of colour on treated modules were less likely to endure many of the everyday psychological traumas that accompanied the general experience of assessment in HE, reported previously by students of colour on other non-modified modules (See sub-section, 'The impact of making assessment racially inclusive for all students', in Chapter 8, for a full summary).

LIMITATIONS OF THE EFFICACY OF THE RIPIAG

The data demonstrates that the intervention has a high efficacy for mitigating against the specific race-based inequities that manifest *within* HE assessment and related practice in a general sense. However, it also shows that the intervention is less effective for mitigating the wider and anti-Black inequities that shape the lived realities of Black heritage students. For example, the intervention's influence does not extend to tackle structural level race-based inequities that can manifest in assessment quality processes, such as those within moderation. Nor does it provide solutions to the influence of a Whitened and Eurocentric curricula (see Campbell et al., 2022), or mitigate the effects of the imbalance in representation between diverse student bodies and Whitened academic faculties, on the assessment performance of students of colour.

Consequently, I recommend that to eliminate RAGs entirely and for *all* students of colour, the academe needs to develop and employ interventions that also and specifically address these wider and anti-Black barriers *in addition* to employing interventions, such as the RIPIAG, which address the more general race-based inequities that are specifically located *in HE assessment practice and pedagogy*.

HOW TO PILOT THE RIPIAG AND WHAT DATA WILL YOU NEED TO MEASURE ITS EFFECTIVENESS?

I conclude this chapter with some instructions for how to pilot the Racially Inclusive Practice in Assessment Guidance Intervention in your own institution.

How to Select Suitable Modules for the Pilot?

The RIPIAG is a pedagogy-focused intervention and not discipline specific. Thus, HEPs are free to select whichever modules on whichever course they would like to test. However, for validity purposes, all modules should consist of at least 25 students with at least 30% of the class consisting of students from global majority backgrounds. HEPs should only test one module per level in a degree programme to ensure reliable comparative data.

What Data Will You Need to Understand and Show the Impact or Effect of the RIPIAG on Practice and Students' Experiences of Assessment?

To capture a holistic understanding of the impact of the RIPIAG, I recommend you adopt a mixed method approach. The two sets of data should include qualitative data gleaned from focus group interviews with students on the sample modules. Where possible, try to disaggregate the experiences captured by disaggregating the focus groups along self-selecting race or ethnicity lines.

The focus group interviews should survey student experiences in relation to (1) their experiences of the assessment changes made on the treated module, (2) how useful they found these changes in supporting their performance in, and literacy of, assessment, and (3) their levels of satisfaction of assessment on treated modules.

Qualitative data should also consist of accounts generated from one-to-one semi-structured interviews or focus groups with module convenors about their experiences of the intervention. Attention should be given to understanding and capturing how it has impacted on their own racial literacy, what changes it has brought to their own practice and what noticeable differences have they witnessed in relation to the students' experiences of assessment on treated modules.

Finally, you will also need quantitative data to capture any reductions in RAGs. This should consist of comparative data in relation to the following (at least):

- The RAG as it relates to students from all backgrounds on the module currently.

- The RAG as it relates to the performance of students from all backgrounds on the module currently, compared to the performance of students in previous iterations (at least 2 years).

- The RAG as it relates to the performance of students from all backgrounds on the module currently compared to the award gaps present on other modules at the same level on the same course.

REFERENCES

Abu Moghli, M., & Kadiwal, L. (2021). Decolonizing the curriculum beyond the surge: Conceptualisation, positionality and conduct. *London Review of Education*, *19*(1), 1–16.

Advance HE. (2021). *Understanding structural racism in UK higher education: An introduction*. AdvanceHE.

Advance HE. (2022). 'New toolkit on embedding mental health into the curriculum', in partnership, in Advance HE magazine. https://www.advance-he.ac.uk/sites/default/files/2022-03/AdvHE_In_Partnership_March_22.pdf. Accessed on June 15, 2022.

Ahmed, F., & Cushing, I. (2021). Banned words and racism in schools. Red Pepper. https://www.redpepper.org.uk/banned-words-and-racism-in-schools/

Akel, S. (2020). *What decolonising the curriculum means*. https://eachother.org.uk/decolonising-the-curriculum-what-it-really-means/. Accessed on January 12, 2024.

Alexander, C. (1996). *The art of being Black*. Oxford University Press.

Andrews, K. (2023). *The psychosis of whiteness*. Penguin.

Andrews, K., & Palmer, A. (2016). *Blackness in Britain*. Routledge.

Archer, L., & Francis, B. (2007). *Understanding minority ethnic achievement: The role of race, class, gender and 'success'*. Routledge.

Arksey, H., & Knight, P. (1999). *Interviewing for social scientists*. Sage.

Arday, J. (2021). *Engaging pedagogically with race and racism BAME awarding gap keynote lecture*. University College London. https://www.youtube.com/watch?v=2S8JUO3M_04

Arday, J., Belluigi, D. Z., & Thomas, D. (2020). Attempting to break the chain: Reimagining inclusive pedagogy and decolonising the curriculum within the academy. *Educational Philosophy and Theory, 53*(2), 1–16.

Arday, J., & Mirza, H. S. (Eds.). (2018). *Dismantling race in higher education: Racism, whiteness and decolonising the academy*. Palgrave Macmillan.

Bhopal, K. (2018). *White privilege. The myth of a post-racial society*. The Policy Press.

Bhopal, K. (2022). 'We can talk the talk, but we're not allowed to walk the walk': The role of equality and diversity staff in higher education institutions in England. *Higher Education, 85*, 325–339.

Bhopal, K. (2023). Critical race theory: Confronting, challenging and rethinking white privilege. *Annual Review of Sociology, 49*, 111–128. https://doi.org/10.1146/annurev-soc-031021-123710

Bhopal, K., & Myers, M. (2023). Elite universities and the making of privilege: Exploring race and class. In *Global educational economies*. Routledge.

Bianco, S. D. (2022). *Reflecting upon the BAME awarding gap at UCL economics*. Reflect Educational Blog. University College London (UCL). https://reflect.ucl.ac.uk/education-conference-2022/2022/03/31/reflecting-about-the-bame-awarding-gap-at-ucl-economics/. Accessed on April 6, 2023.

Bourdieu, P. (1990). *The logic of practice*. Stanford University Press.

Boustani, S. (2023, November 12). Examining exam anxiety: How disadvantage impacts performance. TASO News & Blogs. https://taso.org.uk/news-item/examining-exam-anxiety-how-disadvantage-impacts-performance/?fbclid=IwAR03vPdNf9Vy1eG6idE9sDMUW2MoEuu8394Fa-B4654fgJ-j5lVTly0L6Y8. Accessed on November 12, 203.

Bunce, L., King, N., Saran, S., & Talib, N. (2021). Experience of Black and minority ethnic (BME) students in higher education: Applying self-determination theory to understand the BME attainment gap. *Studies in Higher Education, 46*(3), 534–547.

Burdsey, D. (2022). *Racism and English Football: For Club and Country*. Routledge.

Burgess, S., & Greaves, E. (2013). Test scores, subjective assessment, and stereotyping of ethnic minorities. *Journal of Labour Economics, 31*(3), 535–576.

References

Busby, M. (2020, August 16). BAME children three times more likely to have a Taser weapon used on them by police. *The Guardian*. https://www.theguardian.com/world/2020/aug/16/bame-children-three-times-more-likely-to-have-taser-used-on-them-by-police. Accessed on November 09, 2023.

Butler, D. (2023). *A purposeful life*. Torva.

Byrne, B., Alexander, C., Khan, O., Nazroo, J., & Shankley, W. (2020). *Ethnicity, race and inequality in the UK*. Polity Press.

Campbell, P. I. (2016). *Football, ethnicity and community: The life of an African-Caribbean football club*. Peter Lang.

Campbell, P. I. (2020). *Education training, retirement and career transition for ex-professional footballers: 'From being idolised to stacking shelves'*. Emerald Publishing Limited.

Campbell, P. I. (2021). Now you see 'race', now you don't: The hyper-visibility and hyper-invisibility of race and Covid-19 in political and public health discourse. In T. clarke (Ed.), *Populism, Pandemic and the Media: Journalism in the Age of Covid, Trump, Brexit and Johnson*.

Campbell, P. I. (2022a). *Identifying and 'tackling' racial inequities in HE assessment*. Learning & Teaching Conference. Metropolitan University.

Campbell, P. I. (2022b). 'Pray (ing) the person marking your work isn't racist': Racialised inequities in HE assessment practice. *Teaching in Higher Education*. https://doi.org/10.1080/14660970.2022.2109805

Campbell, P. I. (2023). *"My family's always like, make sure you pray that the person marking your work isn't racist": Identifying and measurably reducing Racial Inequities in HE Assessment*. Forum on Black awarding gaps & decolonisation. Cambridge University.

Campbell, P. I., Ajour, A., Dunn, A., Karavardra, H., Nockels, K., & Whittakers, S. (2022). *Evaluating the racially inclusive curricula toolkit in HE': Empirically measuring the efficacy and impact of making curriculum content racially inclusive on the educative experiences of students of colour in the UK*. University of Leicester: Funded by The Centre for Transforming Access and Student Outcomes in Higher Education. https://doi.org/10.25392/leicester.data.21724658.v1

Campbell, P. I., Hawkins, C., & Osman, S. (2021). *Tackling racial inequalities in assessment in higher education: A multi-disciplinary case study*. University of Leicester: Funded by the Strategic Priorities Fund QR Allocation for Evidence-Based Policy Research. https://le.ac.uk/-/media/uol/docs/institution/tackling-racial-inequalities-in-assessment-in-he-may-21.pdf

Channock, K. (2000). Comments on essays: Do students understand what tutors write? *Teaching in Higher Education*, 5(1), 95–105.

Codiroli-Mcmaster, N. (2021). *Ethnicity awarding gaps in UK higher education in 2019/20*. Advance HE.

Cousin, G., & Cureton, D. (2012). *Disparities in Student Attainment (DiSA)*. Higher Education Academy.

Cramer, L. (2021). Alternative strategies for closing the award gap between white and minority ethnic students. *eLife*, 10, 58971. https://doi.org/10.7554%2FeLife.58971. Accessed on June 30, 2022.

Dal Bianco, S. (2022). *Reflecting about the BAME awarding gap at UCL Economics*. UCL Education Conference 2022: Transforming Assessment. University College London. https://reflect.ucl.ac.uk/education-conference-2022/2022/03/31/reflecting-about-the-bame-awarding-gap-at-ucl-economics/?fbclid=IwAR0KChtDl4DDU4TiAWyPiWuPHhYzEg2PPEPdCr5Y1aQ1-r78_b1Pa1petso#:~:text=To%20summarise%3A%20mixed%20assessment%20strategies,BAME%20students%20and%20their%20needs. Accessed on August 15, 2023.

Darko, N. (2021). Engaging Black and minority ethnic groups in health research: 'Hard to reach'. In *Demystifying misconceptions*. Policy Press.

Dodd, V. (2023, February 19). Black people seven times more likely to die after police restraint in Britain, figures show. *The Guardian*. https://www.theguardian.com/uk-news/2023/feb/19/black-people-seven-times-more-likely-to-die-after-police-restraint-in-britain-figures-show. Accessed on November 09, 2023.

Douglas Oloyede, F., Christoffersen, A., & Cornish CPsychol, T. (2021). *Race equality charter review: Final report*. Advance HE. https://s3.eu-west-2.amazonaws.com/assets.creode.advancehe-document-manager/documents/advance-he/AdvHE_Race%20Equality%20Charter%20Review_1615534497.pdf. Accessed on March 02, 2021.

References

Ellis-Haque, R. (2023, December 28). How can we encourage more prospective first-generation students to apply to university? *Higher Education*. https://www.timeshighereducation.com/campus/how-can-we-encourage-more-prospective-firstgeneration-students-apply-university?fbclid=IwAR1wexY267VDWLnXK Qq4yx1Vi0exQxOEzINlONYt9LQi9apBomEyG50QaUg. Accessed on 28 December, 2023.

Fletcher, T. (2010). "Being inside and outside the field". An exploration of identity, positionality and reflexivity in inter-racial research. In D. Chatziefstathiou & L. Mansfield (Eds.), *Leisure identities and authenticity* (pp. 77–96). LSA Publication.

Fulcher, G.. (2021). Calls to decolonise assessment do students a disservice. https://www.timeshighereducation.com. https://www.timeshighereducation.com/opinion/calls-decoloniseassessment-do-students-adisservice

Fulwood, S., III. (2016, December 15). The United States' history of segregated housing continues to limit affordable housing. americanprogress.org. https://www.americanprogress.org/article/the-united-states-history-of-segregated-housing-continues-to-limit-affordable-housing. Accessed on 12, 2022.

Garcia, C. A., & Duncan, P. (2023, November 29). 'Absolutely shameful' UK ethnicity pay gap persists, figures show. *The Guardian*. https://www.theguardian.com/world/2023/nov/29/absolutely-shameful-uk-ethnicity-pay-gap-persists-figures-show

Garner, S. (2009). *Racisms: An introduction*. Sage.

Gillborn, D. (2006). Critical race theory and education: Racism and anti-racism in educational theory and praxis. *Discourse: Studies in the Cultural Politics of Education*, 27(1), 11–32. https://doi.org/10.1080/01596300500510229

GOV.UK. (2020). *People living in deprived neighbourhoods*. https://www.ethnicity-facts-figures.service.gov.uk/uk-population-by-ethnicity/demographics/people-living-in-deprived-neighbourhoods/latest/. Accessed on July 17, 2023.

GOV.UK. (2023). *Education, skills and training*. https://www.ethnicity-facts-figures.service.gov.uk/education-skills-and-training/. Accessed on February 20, 2024.

Gunaratnam, Y. (2003). *Researching 'race' and ethnicity: Methods, knowledge and power*. Sage.

Herbert, J. (2007). *Negotiating boundaries in the city: Migration, ethnicity, and gender in Britain*. Ashtongate.

Hinton, D. H., & Higson, H. (2017). Large-scale examination of the effectiveness of anonymous marking in reducing group performance differences in higher education assessment. *PLoS One*. https://journals.plos.org/plosone/article?id=10.1371/journal.pone.0182711

Hockings, C. (2010). *Inclusive learning and teaching: A synthesis of the research*. Higher Education Academy. https://www.advance-he.ac.uk/knowledge-hub/inclusive-learning-andteaching-higher-education-synthesis-research

Jacobs, C. (Ed.). (2023). *A new formation: How Black footballers shaped the modern game*. Merky Books.

Joseph-Salisbury, R. (2020). *Race and racism in English secondary schools*. https://www.runnymede trust.org/uploads/publications/pdfs/Runnymede%20Secondary%20Schools%20report%20FINAL.pdf

Khuda, K., & Kamruzzaman, P. (2021). *Our white assessment: Minimising inequality in higher education for international students*. The University of Lincoln Journal of Higher Education Research. ISSN 2516-7561.

King, C. (2004). *Offside racism: Playing the White Man*. Berg.

Kings College London. (2023). *More than a third of people from minority groups in the UK have experienced racist assaults*. Survey Finds News Centre. https://www.kcl.ac.uk/news/more-than-a-third-of-people-from-minority-groups-in-the-uk-have-experienced-racist-assaults-survey-finds. Accessed on February 20, 2024.

Luxon, D., & Zayed, A. (2020, June 16). Cambridge expert explains why 'All Lives Matter' completely misses the point. Cambridgeshire Live. https://www.cambridge-news.co.uk/news/cambridge-news/cambridge-protests-all-lives-matter-18425709?fbclid=IwAR2y7RdDtS-YMcBfRLTdUUztiVW65YP1jad7OG-gZ7jv8Lono1Ifjp0EJXc. Accessed on July 26, 2023.

MacNell, L., Driscoll, A., & Hunt, A. N. (2015). What's in a name: Exposing gender bias in student ratings of teaching. *Innovative Higher Education*, 40(4), 291–303.

Medes, K. (2023). *Postdigitial teens: Gender, violence, and relationships online*. Media Gender Research Group Seminar. University of Leicester. https://www.youtube.com/watch?v=GcH3lka0t18. Accessed on October 11, 2023.

Meer, N. (2021). Discrimination based on your name alone is a stubborn reality in Britain today. *The Guardian*. https://www.theguardian.com/commentisfree/2021/aug/04/name-racial-discrimination-britain-racism-law

Meer, N. (2023). *The cruel optimism of racial justice*. Bristol University Press.

Meer, N., & Chapman, A. (2015). Co-creation of marking criteria: Students as partners in the assessment process. *Business and Management Education in HE*, 1–15. https://doi.org/10.11120/bmhe.2014.00008

Mendes, K. (2023). *'Postdigital Teens: Gender, Violence, and Relationships Online' Media and Gender research group seminar*. University of Leicester. https://www.youtube.com/watch?v=GcH3lka0t18&t=4s. Accessed on December 12, 2023.

Milner, H. R. (2008). Critical race theory and interest convergence as analytic tools in teacher education policies and practices. *Journal of Teacher Education*, 59(4), 332–346.

Moncrieffe, M. (2020). *Decolonising the history curriculum: Euro-centrism and primary schooling*. Cham: Springer.

Morgan, J., & Lambert, D. (2023). *Race, racism and the geography curriculum*. Bloomsbury.

Mountford-Zimdars, A., Sabri, D., Moore, J., Sanders, J., Jones, S., & Higham, L. (2015). *Causes of differences in student outcomes*. ARC Network and The University of Manchester. https://dera.ioe.ac.uk/23653/1/HEFCE2015_diffout.pdf. Accessed on July 14, 2022.

Mukherjee, R., Banet-Weiser, S., & Gray, H. (Eds.). (2019). *Racism: Post race*. Duke Press.

Ofori, M. (2023). Lack of diversity in teaching in England means minority ethnic pupils miss out. *The Guardian*. https://www.theguardian.com/education/2023/aug/29/lack-diversity-teaching-means-minority-ethnic-pupilsengland-miss-out#:~:text=In%20the%20north%2Deast%20of,east%20identified%20as%20black%2DAfrican. Accessed on August 29, 2023.

Rana, K. S., Bashier, A., Begum, F., & Bartlett, H. (2022). Bridging the BAME attainment gap: Student and staff perspectives on tackling academic bias. *Frontiers in Sociology*, 7. https://doi.org/10.3389/feduc.2022.868349

Raven, S. (2022). *The (un)learning of whiteness and its relationship with being-white and developing social justice projects in Physical Education.* PhD Thesis. University of Worcester.

Richardson, J. T. E. (2015). The under-attainment of ethnic minority students in UK higher education: What we know and what we don't know. *Journal of Further and Higher Education, 39*(2), 278–291.

Rollock, N. (2022). *The racial code: Tales of resistance and survival.* Penguin.

Rollock, N., Gillborn, D., & Vincent, C. (2014). *The colour of class: The educational strategies of the Black middle classes.* Routledge.

Sabri, D. (2023). Rethinking causality and inequality in students' degree outcomes' British. *Journal of the Sociology of Education, 44*(3), 520–538.

Saini, S. (2023). The racialised 'second existence' of class: Class identification and (de-/re-)construction across the British South Asian middle classes. *Cultural Sociology, 17*(2), 277–296.

Saleh, A. (2023). Black British literature in the secondary English classroom. *Changing English, 30*(4), 342–358. https://doi.org/10.1080/1358684X.2023.2253178

Sewell, T., Aderin-Pocock, Chughtai, A., Fraser, K., Kakkar, A., Khalid, N., Moyo, D., Muroki, M., Oliver, M., Shah, S., & Olulode, K. (2021). *Commission on race and ethnic disparities: The report.* https://assets.publishing.service.gov.uk/media/6062ddb1d3bf7f5ce1060aa4/20210331_-_CRED_Report_-_FINAL_-_Web_Accessible.pdf. Accessed on November 09, 2023.

Shankley, W., & Finney, N. (2020). Ethnic minorities and housing in Britain. In B. Byrne, C. Alexander, O. Khan, J. Nazroo, & N. Shankley (Eds.), *Ethnicity, race and inequality in the UK: State of the nation.* Policy Press.

Singh, A. (2021). Exploring the racial habitus through John's story: On race, class and adaptation. *The Sociological Review.* https://doi.org/10.1177/03611981211051519

Singh, S., Pykett, J., Kraftl, P., Guisse, A., Hodgson, F., Humelnicu, U. E., Keen, N., Keita, S., McNaney, N., Menzel, A., N'dri, K., N'Goran, K. J., Oldknow, G., Tiene, R., & Weightman, W. (2022). Understanding the 'degree awarding gap' in geography, planning, geology and environmental sciences in UK higher education through peer research. *Journal of Geography in Higher Education.* https://doi.org/10.1080/03098265.2021.2007363. Accessed on June 12, 2022.

Smith, S. V. (2018). The experience of BME commuting students. *Journal of Educational Innovation, Partnership and Change, 4*(1). https://journals.studentengagement.org.uk/index.php/studentchangeagents/article/view/520. Accessed on November 11, 2023.

Solomos, J. (2003). *Race and racism in Britain* (3rd ed.). Palgrave Macmillan.

Song, M. (2015). Does a recognition of mixed race move us toward post-race? In K. Murji & S. Solomos (Eds.), *Theories of race and ethnicity: Contemporary debates and perspectives.* Cambridge University Press.

Sweet, P. L. (2019). The sociology of gaslighting. *American Sociological Review, 84*(5), 851–875.

Takhar, S. (2023). The student voice: Decolonising the curriculum. *Equity in Education and Society.* https://doi.org/10.1177/27526461231192671

Talking Race Podcast. (2021). *Race and Britain with Les Back.* https://podcasts.apple.com/gb/podcast/race-and-britain-with-les-back/id1523519574?i=1000538185277. Accessed on January 02, 2022.

TASO. (2022a). *Summary report: What works to tackle mental health inequalities in higher education.* https://taso.org.uk/wp-content/uploads/Summary_What-works-to-tackle-mental-health-inequalities-in-higher-education_AW-Secured.pdf. Accessed on July 12, 2022.

TASO. (2022b). *The impact of curriculum reform on the ethnicity degree awarding gap.* The Centre for Transforming Assessment and Student Outcomes. https://s33320.pcdn.co/wp-content/uploads/Full-report-the-impact-of-curriculum-reform-on-the-ethnicity-degree-awarding-gap.pdf. Accessed on November 09, 2023.

The Australian. (2023, April 7). *Non-Anglo pay revealed.* https://www.theaustralian.com.au/business/the-deal-magazine/ethnic-pay-gap-workers-from-the-middle-east-africa-asia-face-discrimination/news-story/8c3ab6dd01790bd957e1f141d07e5595#:~:text=According to MindTribes chief executive,largest pay gap of all

Ugiagbe-Green, I., & Ernsting, F. (2022). The wicked problem of B(A)ME degree award gaps and systemic racism in our universities. *Frontiers in Sociology.* https://doi.org/10.3389/fsoc.2022.971923

Wallace, D. (2017). Reading 'race' in Bourdieu? Examining Black cultural capital among Black Caribbean Youth in South London. *Sociology, 55*(1). https://doi.org/10.1177/0038038516643478

Wallace, D. (2019). The racial politics of cultural capital: Perspectives from Black middle-class pupils and parents in a London comprehensive. *Cultural Sociology, 13*(2), 159–177. https://doi.org/10.1177/1749975519839521

Wallace, D., & Joseph-Salisbury, R. (2021). How, still, is the Black Caribbean child made educationally subnormal in the English school system? *Ethnic and Racial Studies.* https://doi.org/10.1080/01419870.2021.1981969

Warikoo, N. K. (2016). *The diversity bargain: And other dilemmas of race, admissions, and meritocracy at elite universities.* University of Chicago Press.

Wright, C. (1992). Early Education: Multiracial primary school classrooms. In D. Gill, B. Mayor, & M. Blair (Eds.), *Racism and education: Structure and strategies.* Sage.

INDEX

Access and Participation Plan (APP), 122
Active Group Marking Exercise (AGME), 75–76, 165, 170
  impact on students' experiences of assessment, 91–96
Assertion, 66
Assessment For Learning (AFL), 156–157
  AFL-based learning principles, 68
Assessments, 7–8
  impact of active group marking exercise on students' experiences of, 91–96
  black students' experiences of, 35, 43, 47
  blueprint for making, 121–124
  British South Asian Students' experiences, 50–52
  coursework, 7
  critical assignment brief and changes in students' lived experiences of, 81–86
  impact of critical assignment schedule on students' lived experiences of, 79–80
  dissertations, 22
  effects of lack of racially and ethnically diverse faculty on, 159
  equitable for students of colour, 162–166
  essays, 20
  exams, 19–20
  experiences of, 23–32
  guidance intervention training workshops for staff, 165–166
  issues with accessing assessment support provided prior to completing, 52–54
  lab reports, 20–21
  literacy, 63
  impact of making, 127–132
  effect of modified active seminar workshops on students' everyday experiences of, 86–91
  open book, 20–21
  practice and students' experiences of, 172
  preferences and access, 152–155
  presentations, 21–22
  process, 86, 98, 119, 129
  quality processes, 171–172
  racialised disparities in accessing curricula and consequences for, 158
  racialised students on modified modules and students of colour on non-modified modules, 97–100
  research projects, 22
  RIPIAG impact on, 167–169
  undergraduate students from South Asian, Black and White racial backgrounds, 152

undergraduate students' lived experiences of, 169–171
white students' experiences in, and preferences for, 19–23

Black British citizens, 48
Black British students' experiences
assessment support processes and practices prior to, and after, completing assignments, 43–47
of different types of assessment, 35–43
Black children, 2
Black law and sociology students, 44–45
Black law students, 37
Black Lives Matter, 142
Black racial backgrounds, assessments experienced differently by undergraduate students from, 152
Black sociology students, 38–40, 154–155
Black students, 42–43
participants, 61
Blueprint for making assessment measurably more racially inclusive, 121–124
Britain
race and progress in, 133–136
racial exclusions in, 115–118
British Bangladeshi, 122
British Black students, 60–61
British East Asian students, 79
British education system, 2–3
British society, 61–62, 128–129
British South Asian biology students, 50–51
British South Asian community, 49
British South Asian students, 60–61
in, and of, different types of assessment, 50–52
experiences of feedback and feed forward, 54–56
issues with accessing assessment support, 52–54

Class
capital, 119–120
currency, 68
habitus, 63
middle class, 69–70
working class, 63
Colonial systems, 4
Colour peers, effective tool for reducing general RAG between students of, 77–79
Conversational approach, 30
Coursework, 38, 51, 61–62, 154, 159–160
Covid-19 pandemic, 135
Criminal justice system, 116–117
Critical Assessment Schedule (CAS), 79–80, 128, 162, 164
Critical Assignment Brief (CAB), 75, 84–85, 164, 169
and changes in students' lived experiences of assessment, 81–86
Critical Assignment Brief, The, 128
Critical Assignment Schedule (CAS), 75
impact on students' lived experiences of assessment, 79–80
Curriculum Consultants, 107–108

Decolonised curricula, 60
Decolonization, 125
Dialogic pedagogy, 87–88
Digital media scholars, 147–148
Dissertations, 22, 40
and research projects, 155
Diversity bargaining, 144

Educators understanding of racial inequities in assessment, 101–105
Epistemological distance, 3
Essays, 38, 51, 154
Ethnically diverse faculty on assessment, effects of lack of, 159
Exams, 152–153
Exercises, 95

Feed forward, British South Asian students' experiences of, 54–56
Feedback, 29–32
  British South Asian students' experiences of, 54–56
  oral feedback, 66, 157
  process, 47, 73, 75
  written feedback, 157
First in their family (FIF), 26
Focus groups, 14
  interviews, 173

Gaslighting, 143–144
Grading process, 38

Higher education (HE), 146
  qualitative impact of RIPIAG on everyday lived experiences of students of colour in, 79
  teachers, staff and lecturers, 166–167
Higher Education Providers (HEPs), 73, 75, 156
  uneven assessment support as facilitator for perceptions of, 159–162

Inclusion, 49
  barriers to inclusion in assessment for racialised undergraduate students, 59–62
  discourse to racially inclusive assessment practice, 105–110
  of exposition, 83–84
Indian heritage British citizens, The, 49–50
Inductive methodological approach, 67–68
Inter-marker variables, 170–171
Interest convergence, 162
Intervention, 162
Interviews, 14

Lab reports, 154

Marginalisation, 67–68
Marking criteria, 76
Marking process, 21, 32–33
Meadow University, 73–75
Metropolitan Police, 143–144
Minority ethnic student, 68
Modified Active Seminar Workshop (MASW), 75–76, 86–87, 164–165, 170
  effect on students' everyday experiences of assessment, 86–91
Modified modules and students of colour on non-modified modules, 97–100
Modified Seminar Workshops, The, 128

Non-anonymised assessments, 154–155
Non-modified modules, 97–100

Office for Students (OFS), 6, 122
One-to-one oral feedback, 66
Open-door forum, 30–32
Oral feedback, 66, 157

Participants, 105, 107
Pattern coding, 14
Physics students, 24–25
Pilot, suitable modules for, 172

Pilot RIPIAG, 172–173
Policymakers, 151
Portfolios, 154
Post-assessment support, 157–158, 161
  approach, 66
  and racialised habitus, 64–67
Postblackness, 147–148
Postracism, 147–149
Pre-assessment guidance, 29–30, 156
Pre-assessment support (PrAS), 46, 62, 64, 155, 157, 160–161
Presentations, 21–22
  and non-anonymised assessments, 154–155
Psychological violence, 143–144
Psychosis of Whiteness, 145

Qualitative assessment, 61–62
Qualitative assignments, 38
Qualitative data, 13, 166, 173
Quality Assurance Agency (QAA), 4–5
Quantitative data, 13, 77, 167–168

Race, 7–8, 131
  inclusion, 133–136
  inequities, 103
  and post-assessment support, 157–158
  and pre-assessment support, 62, 64, 155, 157
  and progress in Britain in new century, 133–136
  race-based barriers, 160
  race-based inequities, 7
Race award gaps (RAG), 6–8, 77, 123, 166
  attempts, 6–7
  RIPIAG impact on assessment performance of students and on, 167–169
  between students of colour and white peers, 77–79
Race Equality Charter, 137

Racial barriers in assessment, 118–121
Racial exclusions in Britain and White Western Nation States, 115–118
Racial inclusion, 103, 126
Racial inequities
  in assessment, 101–105
  in education, 166
Racial literacy
  efficacy of RIPIAG for improving levels of, 166–167
  making measurable improvements to racial literacy of lecturing staff, 124–127
Racialised disparities in accessing curricula and consequences for assessment performance and outcomes, 158
Racialised habitus, 64–67
Racialised students on modified modules and students of colour on non-modified modules, 97–100
Racialised undergraduate students, obvious' barriers to inclusion in assessment for, 59–62
Racially diverse faculty on assessment, effects of lack of, 159
Racially hostile spaces, uneven assessment support as facilitator for perceptions of HEPs as, 159–162
Racially inclusive assessment
  impact of active group marking exercise on students' experiences of assessment, 91–96

Index

contrasting experiences of assessment between racialised students, 97–100
critical assignment brief and changes in students' lived experiences of assessment, 81–86
impact of critical assignment schedule on students' lived experiences of assessment, 79–80
effective tool for helping staff to move from 'inclusion' discourse to, 105–110
effective tool for reducing general RAG between students of colour and white peers, 77–79
effect of modified active seminar workshops on students' everyday experiences of assessment, 86–91
qualitative impact of RIPIAG on everyday lived experiences of students of colour in HE assessment, 79
Racially Inclusive Assessment Guidance, 4–5, 160
Racially Inclusive Practice in Assessment Guidance Intervention (RIPIAG), 4–5, 12, 73, 75–76, 101, 114, 121–122, 127–128, 131, 162, 172
efficacy for improving levels of racial literacy among HE teachers, staff and lecturers, 166–167
impact on assessment performance of students and on RAG at module level, 167–169
impact on students from teachers' perspectives, 110–113
impact on undergraduate students' lived experiences of assessment, 169–171
intervention, 127
intervention training workshops for staff, 165–166
limitations of efficacy of, 171–172
pilot, 172–173
on practice and students' experiences of assessment, 172
qualitative impact of RIPIAG on everyday lived experiences of students of colour, 79
resources, 128
results intervention for making experience of assessment equitable for students of colour, 162–166
as tool for improving educators' understanding of racial inequities in assessment, 101–105
Racially inclusive practice of lecturing staff, making measurable improvements to, 124–127
Racism
covert, 9
gaslighting, 155–156
institutional, 146
microaggression, 49
overt, 9
systemic, 146
Research projects, 22
Russell Group institution, 146

Scaffolded approach, 90–91
Scatter gun approach, 95–96

Science, Technology, Engineering and Mathematics (STEM), 27, 118–119, 153
  STEM-based South Asian students, 56
  STEM-based subjects, 7
Science-based programmes, 65
Sociologist, The, 143–144
South Asian, assessments experienced differently by undergraduate students from, 152
South Asian Britons, 49–50
South Asian physics student focus group, The, 51
South Asian students, 156
Staff, 112–113
  participants, 110
  racially inclusive practice in assessment guidance intervention training workshops for, 165–166
Standard English Tests, 32
State education, 68
Steeper learning curve, 37
Structured sampling method, 9–10
Students, 40–41, 53–54, 90, 157
  impact of active group marking exercise on, 91–96
  frustrations, 47
  effect of modified active seminar workshops on, 86–91
  participants, 62–64, 159
  RIPIAG impact on assessment performance of students and on RAG at module level, 167–169
  stories, 60–61
  from teachers' perspectives, 110–113
  testimonies, 59–60

Students of colour, 97–98
  contrasting experiences of assessment between racialised students on modified modules and, 97–100
  direct and measurable improvements in lived and everyday assessment experiences of, 171
  effective tool for reducing general RAG between, 77–79
  qualitative impact of RIPIAG on everyday lived experiences of, 79
  RIPIAG results intervention for making experience of assessment equitable for, 162–166
Students' lived experiences of assessment
  critical assignment brief and changes in, 81–86
  impact of critical assignment schedule on, 79–80

Talking Race podcast, 133–134
Teachers perspectives, impact of RIPIAG on students from, 110–113
Testimonies, 66, 86–88, 91–92, 97, 101–102, 114, 169
Transforming Assessment and Student Outcomes (TASO), 6–7
Turf Moor Football Ground, 134

UK education system, 61–62
UK Higher Education Providers (HEPs), 4–5
UK housing law, 116
Undergraduate students
  RIPIAG impact on undergraduate students' lived

Index

experiences of assessment, 169–171
from South Asian, Black and White racial backgrounds, 152
Uneven assessment support as facilitator for perceptions of HEPS as racially hostile spaces, 159–162
University of Borne, The, 73–75

Waffly approach, 95–96
White biology students, 20
White British students' experiences of assessment
experiences of assessment support, 23–32
feedback, 29–32
white students' experiences in, and preferences for, different modes of assessment, 19–23

White colonial spaces, 66–67
White peers, effective tool for reducing general RAG between students of, 77–79
White physics students, 20–21
White psychosis, 145
White racial backgrounds, assessments experienced differently by undergraduate students from, 152
White secondary school teachers, 124
White sociology, 24–25
White STEM students, 30, 157
White students, 28–29, 158
White Western Nation States, racial exclusions in, 115–118
Wiseman University, 73–75
Written feedback, 157

Young people of colour, 117

www.ingramcontent.com/pod-product-compliance
Lightning Source LLC
Chambersburg PA
CBHW052021290426
44112CB00014B/2326